MW01226766

WILMA

An Alaska Tale of One Teacher,
Two Teenagers, and Three Wolverines

Dona Agosti

Foreword by Tam Agosti-Gisler

PO Box 221974 Anchorage, Alaska 99522-1974
books@publicationconsultants.com—www.publicationconsultants.com

ISBN 978-1-59433-120-6
Library of Congress Catalog Card Number: 2009913138

Manufactured in the United States of America.

Dedication

To Lino, my husband of 55 years; my children Jan, Ann, Tam, Jon, Tim, Tom, Dave, and Nancy; and the Alaska I love.

October 2009

To Luke,
Enjoy this Alaskan
adventure tale of
yesteryear!
Tam Agosti-Gisler
for
Dona M. Agosti

Acknowledgement

I give special thanks to Bill Moss for use of his wolverine research for this novel. Bill was born in Montana but his parents moved to Alaska when he was nine. He received his BS degree from Rocky Mountain College, Billings (through a full ride baseball scholarship) and his Masters Equivalence in Guidance & Counseling. He taught biology for five years and then served as a guidance counselor for 35 years in both Anchorage and Montana. Bill's wildlife experience was acquired, both from growing up with an uncle who was an outfitter on the Denali Highway in the early 1950s as the road was being built, and from his years as a trapper. Trained in ecology, he loved how the wolverine played such a crucial role in the ecosystem. Bill is retired now and spends his time helping rancher friends with their cattle, wood carving, fishing and enjoying the beauty of Montana.

Foreword

Wilma, An Alaska Tale of One Teacher, Two Teenagers, and Three Wolverines is a story my mother, Dona Agosti wrote in 1969-1970 on her Underwood manual, when typing a manuscript was sometimes more tedious than writing it. Having studied journalism at the University of Minnesota and written a weekly newspaper column while in Berlin during the 1948-49 Airlift, she decided to put her skills to work telling this Alaska story.

Though this is a piece of fiction, the story is built on actual places and what were common Alaska experiences for my family: hiking, hunting, and snow machining as well as science fairs, travel and adventure! Dona was pleased to incorporate the true story of Kay Hitchcock, whom she deeply admired as the quintessential Alaskan woman. Also quite real are the characters Bob Rausch, Alaska Department of Fish and Game; Slim Moore, long-time Alaskan guide and Mr. Jerry McKechnie, Alaska Communications Service. Two other characters have the attributes of one sibling and one very special junior high science teacher. My mother actually did go sheep hunting; we came home empty handed on the trip she arranged for a girlfriend and me! And quite fittingly, Dona actually wrote much of this book at the table of our camping trailer parked along the Caribou Creek featured in this story, while we children played in the woods and water!

Dona tried for quite a while to get this story published, but after numerous rejections, she decided to focus her energies on helping her children undertake rigorous science projects and win science fairs. This manuscript was boxed up and put in a crawl space where it stayed for almost 40 years.

My mother subsequently became an accomplished backpacker and hiking chair of the Mountaineering Club of Alaska. She organized and led many wilderness excursions around the state. One such excursion was a 10-day trek through the Wrangell Mountains, with a group that included the father of a woman who became a well-known Alaska governor! The expertise Dona garnered led to the publication of her non-fiction *how-to* book entitled *The High Country Backpacker*, Winchester Press, 1982.

Although Dona Agosti is now sidelined with Parkinson's disease and a resident of the Anchorage Pioneer Home, I feel it is fitting, during this 50th Anniversary of Alaska's Statehood, to make this wonderful book available to those who would enjoy a good Alaska story of yesteryear.

Tam Agosti-Gisler, October 2009

One

It was the Friday evening of an Alaska February way back in the alder-covered foothills where the Talkeetna Mountains meet the Matanuska Glacier. A female wolverine who did not know her name was Wilma luxuriated in a natural sauna. The snow-laden tree roots above provided just the right heating arrangement for her den. While the trails of vapor rising from her site might be a dead giveaway, the likelihood of her observation was as remote as the location. An animal worry crossed her mind briefly. Had she heard a foreign sound several times this winter? But hadn't she also enjoyed some special meals courtesy of an unknown host? Always it was necessary to be cautious of course—just a simple matter of nosing a branch into the waiting jaws and snap, the meal was hers. There was a smell nearby that she did not know, but no harm had come her way. Yet, she must be careful.

Emerging from the dark recesses of her den, she reared back on her hind legs, wafted the air cautiously then settled back on her haunches for a quick tongue bath. The snow-heavy spruce branch above her cracked and Wilma snapped to attention, white hairs bristling, bushy tail agitatedly describing a circle. Investigation completed and satisfied that no intruders had invaded her territory, she bounded off through the snow leaving delicate paw designs behind her. Wilma loved snow. Her large padded feet provided natural snowshoes as she loped through three or four feet of the powdery stuff. Wilma, being a lady, would like to have known that she presented a rather attractive picture for all the world, much like a ruffle on a Sunday dress: rich brown velvet fur along her back, unusually white stripes along her sides, a small bear-like face, tiny ears, and the odd but distinctive white tufts under her neck. Her coat would deteriorate during spring rubbing time, but now she glowed like all pregnant ladies. In the way of the enceinte, she knew that good diet was essential and she hastened to the carrion site. Reaching the summit of a rise overlooking the frozen lake below, Wilma once more assumed a hind-leg stance, swiveled her neck sniffing all the while, then, satisfied, bounced through the frozen muskeg humps to the lake's edge. There she found a moose kill made and vacated by wolves and she busily commenced gnawing where she had left off yesterday. Her sharp fangs made short work of the frozen haunch. Ever cautious, she constantly flashed upright for an inspection sniff or two, and satisfied, resumed her meal. Though she had long ago marked this prize, to the obvious consternation of the wolf pack, she now purchased further insurance. With a deft twist, she maneuvered her rear over the carrion, wiggled expertly and ejected the contents of musk glands. That should fix any visitors! Sated and happy, she galloped off intent on an inspection of her territory.

It was the Friday evening of an Alaska February when fifteen-year-old Tom Lerner pulled on his thermal underwear. Over that he stretched, first east then west, a white tee shirt. Then blue jeans. In haste, he maneuvered into a fluorescent orange jump suit. Pawing through the top drawer of his dresser, he found a pair of wool socks exactly where his mother said they'd be. He put them on propped midair and hopping on one foot. Then he examined the mess on his closet floor.

"Mom. Mom. MOM! Did Dad borrow his mukluks from me?"

The kitchen of the house replied, "Try his closet. He used them hunting last weekend."

"Oh. I forgot."

Tom inhaled. "Mmmmm. It does smell good. Hey Ma, what do you think of my jump suit?" His insulated form slid into the dinette corner.

"I know one thing," said Mary Lerner. "If I were a wolverine, I'd see you before you saw me." The tall, blonde lady grinned back at the tall, blond boy.

Tom found the footwear down the hall in his father's closet. Let the Eskimos and Athabascans argue over who could make a better mukluk; either kind bought frostbite insurance. Back in his room, Tom snatched up his ski mitts and knitted facemask and hurried to the kitchen.

"Wonder why Mr. Marx is so late," he mumbled.

"It's five and he said he'd pick you up at 5:15," his mother corrected. "Sit down and eat some hot stew. Wait 'til you get in those cold hills. You'll want more than hot stew."

It was the Friday evening of an Alaska February in her fourteenth year and Pam Walker was sailing into a happening. She had decided that neat Mr. Marx was just about top man on her totem pole. She wondered what this evening would have been like if he had not thought up that dreamy contest in Biology class and if she, Pam Walker, might not this very minute be waiting to depart on an adventure. She remembered way back in the school year when Mr. William Marx was spouting on about mammals and mustelids as fast as the ninth grade class of Romig Junior High could take notes. Eventually they steered him onto a firsthand Alaska biology lecture about wolverines. Mr. Marx was writing a Science Foundation paper, but most of his information came from personal experience as a trapper. The kids were hanging over their desks when he told about one hairy meeting with William on the trail. Oh yes, the class wanted to name this particular wolverine "William the Wily One," but Mr. Marx said the alliteration was a subtle as a wolverine's scent, and besides he was a she. Pam wondered about that scent business.

The kids started the question game to keep Mr. Marx on the subject of wolverines and off the drier stuff about mustelids and ecology and all that.

Tom Lerner was fastest: "Mr. Marx, why don't you take the class on a field trip to your trap line?"

After Mr. Marx had shushed the affirmative vote, he explained, "There are 9,000 reasons why not. I cover 25 miles and 100 traps on that line, in the dead of a winter night at 45 below zero on a snow machine. Now let's see those hands again!"

A few diehards persisted. He shrugged with a laugh in that way of his, took off his black-rimmed glasses, and then put them back on again. The kids knew they had him measured when he went to the blackboard and erased all that day's junk.

"Okay, wise ones, here's your answer. We will each do a research paper."

GROAN.

"The paper will be a college-type, Grade A, top student piece of work and it will concern itself with a little animal called the wolverine."

GROAN, GROAN.

"You will have until after Christmas vacation to complete it. Then, my eager students, a select committee will judge them—and I can suggest now that one judge might be a 40-year Alaskan guide, one might be a biologist from the Alaska Department of Fish and Game, and one just might be me. We will select two winners."

Pam Walker could stand the suspense no longer: "Where does the field trip come in?"

"Brain cells in suspension today, Pam? Why don't you make one of those brilliant, logical deductions of yours and see what you come up with?"

"Do you really mean it? Will the two winners go with you on the trap line?" Pam brilliantly and logically deduced.

"Great to have you back with us, Pam. You are correct."

With that the class went into an uproar and Mr. Marx hoped the principal wasn't making one of his hall tours about then. One thing he knew—his little-known, highly maligned trapline acquaintance was about to be discovered by a certain Seventh Period Junior High School class.

Pam pulled herself from the memory of that day and for the 9,000th time checked the leather laces on her mukluks. "Mother, I hope these darn things are as warm as they say. I used three months of babysitting money to buy them. Are you sure the label on the socks said wool, because I'll freeze a foot and they'll saw it off like they did in that movie at school. Where in the world are Mr. Marx and Tom, do you think they can't find the house? Mom this jump suit is too big…"

Pam's mother, after opening her mouth to reply to each of her daughter's questions, decided to plunge in with a comment of her own: "It's quite a relief to see you in something a little less tight than those jeans you girls pour yourselves into these days. Besides you need some airspace for warmth. Are you sure you have your brother's thermal underwear on?"

"Nope, I borrowed Dad's—the ones you shrunk. I hope he doesn't come home before I leave, because I have his moosehide gloves, too. They're really toasty warm."

"Just don't take them off for too long at 45 below, and keep your face covered with your mask when you're on that snow machine. I don't need a frostbitten female in this house along with all my other problems."

A girl squeal punctuated the air: "Mom, they're here! Oh doesn't Tom look absolutely riotous in that jump suit?" She didn't wait to see her mother raise a quizzical eyebrow.

Flinging the army surplus pack over one arm and jamming the sleeping bag into the other, she called a bubbling "Bye Mom" in the general direction of that long-suffering one, sailed through the door, raced down the snow-lined driveway… and promptly sat down hard on her bottom—right at the feet of the jump-suited Tom. He gallantly assisted her to her feet, then looked up as Mrs. Walker called from the lighted doorway:

"You forgot your mask and gloves, dear."

Mr. Marx, bemused, extricated his parka-clad form from beneath the wheel of the green Chevrolet super truck and walked to the door of the suburban Anchorage home. Accepting the sundries from Mrs. Walker, he asked, "You aren't worried about her, are you?"

"Maybe a little, but I have a great deal of confidence in you, and besides, she'd probably leave home if I said she couldn't go now. There should be some reward if all that moaning and groaning over a report meant anything." She added, "I see you have the snow machine in the back of the pickup—I hope it's a good one. I have an aversion to frozen bodies."

"I just tuned up the engine and it's in fine shape. In my six years of trapping I've never had any real trouble. Maybe a spark plug or broken belt, but I've got extra parts along and a good tool kit and I can take care of most problems. Besides, it wouldn't be impossible to walk out if the machine really broke down. Don't worry—you've got a daughter who uses her head for something besides growing hair."

"I really won't—it's a wonderful opportunity to know the real Alaska. I'm just a little bit envious. Good luck and have fun! We'll see you back late tomorrow, right?"

As they edged out of the driveway, Pam snugly ensconced between two other shapeless forms in the front seat of the pickup. Mrs. Walker did indeed sense a glimmer of adventure ahead. And she was happy for her daughter.

She stood at the window long after the tail lights of their truck had disappeared in the early winter darkness musing on the man to whom she had entrusted her daughter. Here indeed was a teacher. His sturdy athletic frame accented his great love affair with the Alaska scene. When he removed his dark-rimmed glasses, the pedagog disappeared and a young man with brown eyes, prematurely gray-speckled brown hair and flashing grin appeared. Probably to amuse his teenage students he wore his sideburns long in the current mode. She guessed him to be about thirty, but his ancient maturity was that born of insight and keen understanding of human nature. Her thoughts went back to one day when she had visited his class. He had both a strong command of his subject and an uncanny rapport with the students. The class was alive, alert and responsive as they scrambled to take notes and simultaneously arm themselves for the always-compelling finger pointed mid-brain.

Musing further, she wondered about her daughter's stamina when confronted with trapline realities. Here was a girl capable at once of startling logic, extreme femininity and intense compassion. She remembered their Alaska Highway trip to Minnesota last summer. They had vacationed for a month at a lakeshore cabin. Pam's small brothers, unfamiliar with snakes because there were none in Alaska, had stoned a small, garter variety. Gently, Pam carried the victim to the house, wrapped a band-aid about its bleeding middle and returned it to the woods where it lumpily slithered off. She hoped Pam could maintain the proper degree of professional woodswoman on the trapping trail. She'd better or two males were in for it.

Turning absently away from the window, Mrs. Walker walked to the sink, plunged her hands into warm dishwater and was happy for her daughter.

Two

It took Pam less than two miles to ascertain that she was Target For The Trip. Mr. Marx and Tom fell all too naturally into Tormenter Position, a fact of life readily recognizable to Female With Brothers. Perhaps the latter was reason for her daft fielding of jibes and complete ease though surrounded.

Mr. Marx pitched the first ball: "Pam, did you take a good look at yourself in that jump suit? That color reminds me of the dirty water in the Science Lab aquarium—the one you kids always forget to change."

Tom added, "I was thinking it looked more like that frog specimen in the jar. Where did you find that wild color anyway?"

"In the same store you found that neurotic orange you've got on," retorted Pam. "You realize only crazed extroverts would select a color that wild. At least my lime green is subtle."

The power struggle proceeded as Mr. Marx threaded his way through the Anchorage traffic and onto the Glenn Highway leading out of the city. Gradually on-coming headlights and city street lights thinned. The car's interior seemed snug and warm, probably exaggerated by the knowledge of zero weather without; the car radio turned to KHAR alternated traffic reports with relaxing music. It was to this deplorable state of affairs that Tom turned his attention.

"Hey, Mr. Marx. How come you've got that creepy station on instead of KENI? Why don't you switch to some real music?"

"Because I don't want my brains rattled loose. But just to show you what a good guy I am, I'll alternate stations. Fifty miles of KHAR and five miles of KENI."

And with that he switched stations. An unmistakable jumble electronic discord filled the car, and the two teenagers smiled appreciatively. They could do little more. The sound was all-enveloping. It helped little that the tune was followed by a popular singer, plaintively wailing the same two lines ten times.

"Five miles are up," said the driver, pushing a station button. It was his turn to breathe appreciatively as a tune from Camelot caressed the eardrums. And for fifty miles, music served as pleasant background to conversation rather than total replacement of it.

The conversation inevitably turned to the subject of the day, and much research and many pages wiser, the two students were eager to discuss the object of their trip—the wily wolverine. They had eventually succumbed to practical suggestion and "William" had become "Wilma."

"All right, you two hoods. Since this is a Biology Field Trip, how about a little review. Tom, a bit of mammology, please."

Tom replied in mock sing-song: "The wolverine is a mustelid found in the arctic regions of Europe, North America, and Russia. The American variety is known as Gulo Luscus—Glutton, half blind—loosely translated. I think he's hungrier in Europe because they call him Gulo Gulo or straight glutton. This legend about the wolverine's voracious appetite is one of the many fairy tales perpetrated about the wolverine. Say, Mr. Marx, I sound just like you don't I?"

"Exactly," Mr. Marx replied drily. "Please continue, Pam," he continued with mock classroom severity.

"The wolverine is a carnivore—that's meat eating to you—and gold miners near Fairbanks helped prove that he existed in the Pleistocene Age when they dug up the skulls. He is sometimes called a skunk-bear. He looks like a small bear and smells like a skunk, but not always. He doesn't squirt stuff when he's mad like a skunk does, but uses the junk from these anal glands to mark territory—like over a caribou kill or just to mark out his territory."

"I might interrupt here," said Mr. Marx. "The scent from these glands is powerful and frankly, awful; the stuff looks something like dirty yellow mustard. I use it on my traps to attract wolverines. It is quite important when removing these glands from a dead animal that you do not break the membrane—or you'll be sorry."

"To continue," Pam said patiently, "the wolverine mates in about August or September and has her babies about nine months later. But here's a funny thing—the fertilized egg just lies around loose in her uterus for a couple months, then attaches to the wall and starts developing. Same as the weasel and the marten. And we don't know much about the baby history because so few have been observed— especially here in Alaska."

"I'll make a small confession here," said Mr. Marx. "I observed Wilma's den site last February and could easily have seen some kits if I hadn't been so soft about tearing the den apart. There's a Dr. Knutson, I think his name is, in Whitehorse, Canada… he has some animals in captivity and feels you can't learn too much from captive animals. Guess I was worried the kits would die if I removed them from their natural environment."

Pam was quick to answer. "Too bad you didn't read Peter Krott's book. It's called *Demon of the North* and he spent a lifetime taming and writing about wolverines in Finland. He called them tupus. Guess you're right though… he had a rough time keeping the babies alive. Know what? You have to feed the babies just right. They need boiled milk diluted with water to lukewarm temperature just like a baby. And, this is a riot, you have to massage their tummies and their bottoms, because that's what the mother does with her tongue after they've nursed."

A startled silence filled the truck cab. Pam flushed, but knowing she'd scored points, she plunged on.

"And Mr. Krott proved that wolverines could be trained to the leash and tamed as pets."

"That was a good job of researching, finding that book, Pam. I haven't read it myself. Okay, Tom, quit throwing a fit and say it. What else?"

"She forgot to say 91% of the Alaska wolverine population breeds annually and they have from one to six kits."

"It's called dropping kits," said Mr. Marx.

"Well anyway, they have—they *drop*—their kits in about February or March. Funny thing. You know the State of Michigan has a football team named the Wolverines, and they haven't been seen for a hundred years in Michigan."

"Who? The football team?" asked Mr. Marx.

"I mean it. There are a few wolverines in the northern states and Canada, but Alaska has the most."

"Brings up a sticky subject, Tom. For years they had a bounty system here. They thought wolverines along with wolves and coyotes were responsible for the diminishing moose, sheep and caribou populations. Last year the Legislature repealed the bounty act. Really what they did was give the Board of Fish and Game authority to specify game units in which bounties would no longer be paid. The one we're trapping in today is a no-bounty unit. I'm for it 100% because it sure cut out the big operators who were taking large numbers of wolves in aircraft. By the way, when you collect bounty on an animal, you turn in just the legbone and you can sell the hide. If you've handled it well, and the paws are still there, you can get as much as $60.00; if it's simply a pelt, a furrier will probably give you $35.00 for it. All depends on the market and who you sell it to here in Alaska or Outside."

"I remember reading about some kind of hassle a few years back. Why was everybody so fired up? Man, you shoulda read some of those letters to the editor," remembered Tom.

"Game management is a highly emotional issue in Alaska. There are so many hunters and outdoorsmen here. That's why the big hassle. But here's basically what it was all about. You might say there are three points of view in this thing—one is the organized conservationist, another is the hunter, and another is the professional biologist or wildlife official. By organized conservationist I mean some national organization, usually operating from outside the state, which is firmly convinced that we Alaskans know absolutely nothing about conservation and are all set to slaughter every animal here to extinction. Their theory is that there should be no hunting at all. Now this is the extreme point of view of course, and there are the more moderate conservationists who believe in good game management. Now on the opposite end, we can put another extreme, the hunter who believes that the only good wolf or wolverine is a dead one—or the old timer who, because of Alaska's sparse population, has seen no diminishing of game in his lifetime and resents any kind of control. Now his point of view is extreme, too. Then, maybe we can put in the middle the professional biologists in the Alaska Department of Fish and Game who do a great deal of research attempting to reach a balance. Here's how you could sum up their work: they are simply trying to maintain a static population of any type of animal which is in balance with its range."

Tom broke in, "What's range?"

"That's what the animal feeds on—with moose or caribou, it's the lichen or other browse; with animals like wolves or wolverines which are meat eating, it's the small animals such as mice, hare or shrews."

"Isn't it true, Mr. Marx, that wolves and wolverines usually attack only the easiest animals they can take, like the old or diseased or crippled?" asked Pam.

"Not always, and that brings up another point. They will often attack the young sheep or calves. But that is necessary too. Even in domestic management of herds, some young are harvested while others are maintained to replace the maturing animals. Remember that animals of this category don't breed until they are yearlings, so actually the first year is a wasted year if you want to be blunt about it. In the true Balance of Nature where man is not involved, some young always perish. That's why I say we manage wildlife best when we copy nature. Guess you could say that's a trapper's point of view crossed with the biologist."

"One thing that really got me was the way Native Americans feared the wolverine. They called him a carcajou," Pam continued.

"Carca-who?" queried Tom.

Mr. Marx explained, "That's the name the Eskimos and Indians from here to everywhere have given the wolverine. They believe he had mystic powers beyond human or animal capability. In reality, he's just a craft, wary animal and quite shy when you observe him. I also believe he is basically a scavenger, not a predator or marauder as so many trappers and even naturalists have claimed."

"How was that again?" asked Pam.

"Simple. Predator means an animal that preys on or feeds on other animals. A scavenger or marauder depends on other kills, and does little of his own hunting."

"Got it."

Pam noticed they were passing through Palmer; the small farming community twinkled with early evening traffic. A few miles later, the truck began to climb above the frozen Matanuska River Valley. The moon was almost full and the riders caught an occasional glimpse of the awesome valley far below. As they rounded curves, the headlights showed snow walls threatening to block their way, but always there was more road ahead. Once Pam saw a frozen lake on her right and was startled when she realized it was Long Lake, a favorite summer stop for swimming and eating, now a stranger dressed in winter white. They continued to climb, Mr. Marx throwing the four-wheel drive truck into second gear when necessary. Pam handed out gum for the ear-popping descent somewhere between Cascade and Hick's creeks, and she was so busy caring for her ear drums and passing coffee to the driver that she was startled to hear that they were almost there. She glanced at her watch. It was 9:00 pm, which in her teenage opinion was a real cool time to depart for an adventure. Mr. Marx slowed the truck and turned into a wayside area cleared by highway snow plow crews.

"Come on, kids. All out."

"All out to where?" Tom protested.

"Didn't you see that cabin down the road?" said beady-eyed Pam, glad for once that she hadn't missed something.

It took moments for their eyes to adjust to the night light after the car lights had been turned off. The moon shivered alone in the coal black sky. They didn't hesitate long before plunging down the slope, sinking mid-thigh where the snowplow had pushed snow over the hillside. A yellow path of welcome reached out to them from the cabin window below.

"For heaven's sake, it's painted red," spoke Pam. "And look at that darling cache beside it—it's got a screen around the top instead of logs. Look, he doesn't have the metal piece on the legs. For cat's sake why not?"

"For cat's sake there should be," quipped Tom, not intending to be outpunned.

"Let's ask Henry and avoid frostbite," answered Mr. Marx.

Mr. Marx pounded on the door, then tried the handle. Peering in he saw Henry TwoChiefs rustle sleepily from beneath the warmth of a caribou hide.

"Don't get up, Henry. I'm going right out on my trap line. Got two assistants with me tonight—Pam, Tom, this is Henry TwoChiefs."

Pam eyed the glistening naked shoulders of the half-asleep Athabascan Indian and modestly averted her gaze. "Hi," she said, and walked over to the water pail on the sink. She certainly was thirsty, she explained, whereupon half a dipperful dribbled down her front.

Tom, enjoying her discomfort immensely, became Man-in-Complete-Charge and greeted Henry. "Glad to meet you, Henry. Hear you're a great trapper."

"Mind if I poke up this Yukon stove, Henry?" asked Mr. Marx. "I want it to be going when we come back in five or six hours."

"Don't worry," mumbled Henry from the depths. "I have it nice and warm when you come back."

"Appreciate your hospitality, Henry. I brought you some fresh vegetables and bread from Anchorage."

"Here. Catch." Pam threw a sandwich to Mr. Marx.

"That was some fast cooking, Pam."

"Yup. Right out of my pack. Here's yours, Tom."

"Thanks. Henry, think you can stand some of Pam's cooking?"

Pam handed a sandwich to Tom. He took it over to Henry in bed.

After the snack, the three climbed back to the highway. They watched Mr. Marx untie the nylon rope and pull the Polaris snow machine forward. It dropped to the ground like a skier hitting the slopes. While they lashed the trap box to the rear end of the machine, the teacher thought about the temperature. The thermometer outside Henry's cabin showed ten below and the full moon told him it would go much lower before the 12-mile run was over. He wondered for a minute whether he was entirely wise in taking kids into a situation as potentially dangerous as this. He shrugged off the momentary fear, knowing that his passengers were level-headed kids as Alaskan as their birth certificates.

He snapped the coiled rope of the snow machine forward. No response. Repeatedly the sluggish motor coughed and died. Finally, it sparked to life and idled smoothly.

"You'd better," he muttered to the machine.

"What in the world is that box for?" asked Pam. She nodded towards the square container attached to the machine.

"Any trapper would know it's a trap box," teased her teacher. "And before you ask any more great questions, that fiberglass sled is an Akeo."

"Yes, I know. It's the modern version of what the Laplanders called an Ackya and theirs is used as a reindeer sledge," piped Pam. She was enjoying her exclusive knowledge gained from the one book her adversaries had not read.

William Marx made a final check. Twenty-two rifle, ammunition, first aid kit, thermos bottles of consommé and coffee, sandwiches, candy bars, extra gas, tools, extra parts, bait matches. He inspected his charges and saw that each was wearing a facemask and gloves. Pam had added a fake fur hat over her mask and the effect was as funny as she intended it to be. He could almost see her eyes twinkle through the slits. Those masks always reminded him of faces on a totem pole.

"It's a good thing you kids are diffcrent colors. I'd have a tough time telling you apart."

Pam giggled.

"On second thought, guess I wouldn't," noted the teacher.

"We're off," roared the driver, and the Polaris responded enthusiastically. "Grab the sled and follow me up the highway to the trail!" Pam and Tom obeyed and they soon crossed the highway into a small clearing. Tom quickly tied the sled to the machine, then hopped aboard the trap box seat. That left the sled for Pam, who believed now that she really was destined for a *ride*. Doggedly, and not to be out-maneuvered, she assumed the stance of Queen Victoria, daintily picked her way to the sled, and regally deposited her royal body aboard. Mr. Marx gunned the motor, which in turn jerked the sled, which in turn rearranged a royal body flat on her backside in the snow.

The royal entourage apologetically hastened to her side and redeposited the flailing body aboard the Akeo. Before she could re-join them front side, the driver roared off into the moonlight. It was a while before they could stop laughing and attend to business.

Tom yelled above the roar of the machine, "How does this trail happen to be so wide and who owns it?"

"Most of the trails in these hills have been hunting paths for years. Even though they are homesteaded over, the Bureau of Land Management—that's the Department of the Interior—retains the right of public access… sort of like grandfather's rights you'd call it."

He continued, "My first trap is right up the line. First I thought it'd be a waste of time setting them too near the highway because those trucks make some wild noises descending that Caribou Creek hill… sounds like Sunday on a rifle range when they backfire. But it doesn't seem to bother the animals at all."

Partly because it was so difficult to hear and partly because Tom found himself succumbing to the awe of the Northland, the trappers were silent now. Tom turned around to Pam and pointed to the moon. It had a haunting luminescence about it. But she was too busy staying aboard the sled to concentrate. Mr. Marx turned off the snow machine lights. The stark contrast of white snow and black night created a twilight illusion. Tom thought he'd have no trouble seeing his way through the forest, but when he tried to read his watch, he knew it was an illusion. A light snow had fallen in the past day or two, but tracks of a previous snow machine run ribboned softly ahead of them. Mr. Marx expertly threaded his way through the spruce and alder shadows, around a fallen tree, into and out of ravines, then braked to a stop. He walked quickly off the trail to a trap and found it still baited but empty. Pam and Tom gathered near and watched with interest as he snapped the trap shut and showed it to them.

"This is a double spring No. 4 Victor. I use offal and scent for bait."

"Repeat that please," said Pam.

"Offal and scent."

"Yes, I know the scent is awful, but what's the other stuff?"

"Wise girl. It comes from a butcher shop and it's any kind

of meat trimmings wild or otherwise that I can get my hands on."

He turned back to the trap, expertly changed the bait, and because he was setting for a lynx, omitted the wolverine scent. Pam examined the trap more closely and noticed the trapper had built a sort of half tent around it.

"Why did you prop those spruce boughs around the trap?" she asked.

"So he uses the door… see, here's the 'dog'—that's trapper's language for the bait-holder, and I put a small pile of twigs in front of it. That way the animal steps over it and into the trap. Back here, behind the trap, is where I put the scent when I'm baiting for wolverine."

"Why do you have such a long chain attached to the trap?" asked Pam.

"Watch." He threaded the chain through one side of the tent then walked around to the outside and fastened it to an alder pole a few feet away.

"Why the Rube Goldberg bit?" asked Tom.

"Easy. This way he can't wander off with the trap or worse yet tear off a paw trying to get out."

Pam turned from her inspection to see Mr. Marx already astride the machine and Tom hopping on behind him. She raced to the sled and braced herself as they shot forward.

The second trap was not so routine. Mr. Marx saw it first.

"I think we've got us a lynx. Get off the trap box, Tom, I need the rifle." He slipped a shell into the chamber, lifted the gun to his shoulder, and fired. The animal dropped over with a snarl.

"This is a beautiful pelt," he said, examining the carcass. "Wish I could have got here before she damaged that right foot."

He released the trapped foot, grasped two legs in each hand and swung the animal into the trap box. But not before Pam had looked the lynx straight into its sightless eyes.

"Oh, that poor lynx. I hope he didn't suffer."

"I don't think he's been here long, Pam," sympathized Mr. Marx.

The next three traps were empty, but still baited. After inspecting the meat in each, Mr. Marx was off and running.

"I get the impression that speed is important here," Tom drolly commented.

"Got to stay warm some way," replied the operator.

The next trap provided a story to tell grandchildren.

They stopped and Mr. Marx scrambled off into the alder. When they caught up, they gasped, because dead and gone to his glory was the animal they had done nothing but talk about for months—a magnificent male wolverine.

"He's bigger than I thought," Pam ventured.

"You're right about that, Pam. An average animal weighs around 25 to 30 pounds. I would guess this one runs about 40. And look here, kids. He's chewed part of his paw off. When the trap snaps shut, it cuts off circulation and that part of the foot immediately freezes, so he chews it off hoping to free himself at the same time. Another thing, notice how he fought this trap. The chain is wrapped around his rib cage. That's probably why he's dead. The chain restricted his breathing. It's unusual to find dead animals in a trap."

"He's so cute," offered Pam.

"Correction. He *was* so cute," countered Tom.

"Tom, I'm running low on wolverine scent. Will you help me remove the scent glands from this animal? Good dissection experience. Shouldn't be too difficult because he's not frozen solid yet. *But, man, be careful.* Don't break the membrane on those sacs or you'll be persona non grata for six months."

"He's already unacceptable. Don't compound the felony," Pam implored. "Mr. Marx, you can't… you don't really mean you're going to let that incompetent mess around with scent glands, do you?"

About then the motor died on the snow machine and Mr. Marx jogged back to the trail to restart the engine. For some reason, it because obstinate, and it was five minutes or more before the engine would idle on its own. An anguished call reached his ears and he adrenalined into action.

"Help! Help! Mr. Marx! This is terrible. Quick. Help!"

Then the teacher stopped, fully aware of the sight which would meet his eyes when he reached the screamer. He pushed aside a branch and walked slowly up to Tom. Breathing solely through his mouth, he managed to comment at the same time, "Now you know what I mean."

Never had he seen a more crestfallen, totally shaken youth. The musky odor of wolverine scent was everywhere, and winters later, Pam would smell it in her sleep. More obnoxious than skunk, more penetrating than ether—it was an odor one would never forget.

There was nothing to do now but finish the job. Mr. Marx removed his gloves and parka and set them off to the side, far off. Tom gingerly held the carcass while Mr. Marx cut wide around the punctured glands. He broke off an alder branch and cautiously lifted the offensive things out. Pulling slowly back, he aimed, then tossed them as far as he could throw and sat down to breathe through his mouth once more.

"Next time you'd better let me do it," Miss Cook-of-the-Walk rejoined. "Dad showed me how to cut the insides out of a moose when we were hunting and I didn't go busting any lungs or intestines on the way out. You have to be coordinated, Tom, just coordinated."

When she saw that she had mortally wounded his masculine vanity, she added, "But that's all right, Tom. We all make mistakes occasionally. Some of us just make bigger ones." And Pam noted the incident in her Book of Life as she handed Tom a Wash-n-Dri from the recesses of her backpack. She wished now that she had brought that plastic squeeze bottle of cologne.

———•◦•———

About a mile or so up the trail Mr. Marx swung right to a ridge overlooking one of several little lakes in the area. This is where he had observed the wolverine den site for his National Science Foundation report; although he had played down the possibilities of a sighting, he was secretly hoping to put his mustelid friend on display for his youthful tourists. Since a wolverine is perpetually wary, and never one to greet guests unless trapped, Mr. Marx stopped the machine and shut off the motor. Cautioning the two to silence, he motioned for them to follow. They silently plodded through the fluffy snow, watching for giveaway tracks or scat. When their guide threw himself to the ground behind a fallen tree, they jolly well knew they'd better follow suit.

"I don't see a thing," whispered Pam through a face full of snow.

Mr. Marx was too excited to be clever right then.

"Look across the ravine in that patch of moonlight. See that dark hole beneath the roots of that round-topped spruce… see the steam rising from it—that's the den site and she must be there or there wouldn't be so much vapor. I wonder if she's dropped her kits or if she's still gravid."

"Please, Mr. Marx," pleaded Pam in a tiny voice. "Will you translate?"

"What? Oh you mean gravid. That's pregnant."

"It would be nice if you said so," she whispered.

That sat almost rigid for twenty-two minutes by the watch, moving only to pass the binoculars. They hardly dared breathe when Wilma the Wily One entered backstage, wafted the air cautiously, then commenced her morning ablutions. This completed, she seemed to remember that pregnant ladies must eat well and loped delicately through the moonlit snow to her cache. The downwind audience saw that she need no tools to complete her breakfast of moose haunch.

"I thought *Gulu* meant glutton," whispered Pam. "Creeps, Tom eats more than that on a Coke break!"

Wilma must have caught the sounds of a *homo sapiens* because she moved quickly off from the carrion site, bolted upright, sniffed, and then bounded off in the direction from which they had just come.

"Guess our wolverine watching is over for this trip," said Tom. "But I was beginning to coagulate anyway."

"Wasn't she just beautiful?" breathed Pam.

"I kinda feel that way, myself, Pam," said Mr. Marx.

They thoughtfully plowed back to the machine and climbed aboard.

"Rigor Mortis has set in," said Pam. "Let's move."

The driver veered left and they wound their way between two high ridges. They came out onto a large snow-covered lake crisscrossed with animal tracks. Mr. Marx yelled that Pinochle Creek was not too far ahead. They could feel ice fog prickle the face when they descended into a gully, and Mr. Marx noticed that the machine was responding more sluggishly as the temperature crept downward. He guesstimated it to be about 15 or 20 below now. He stopped the machine, and checked the last trap.

"Think we'll call it a night. What've we got… three lynx and two wolverine? Pretty good for only half the line. I'll let my brother-in-law hit the rest of them tomorrow. You kids got a good idea what trapping is all about now?"

"I'd rather talk about it back at the cabin," said Pam.

"It'll take me a month to thaw out," said Tom.

The teacher swung wide and began the return trip over the trail they had just covered.

"Hang tough. We'll be back soon."

He did not know that nature had plans of her own.

Three

The machine sped on. It was almost three in the morning and if Pam hadn't been so cold she might have been sleepy. Her bones ached and she could no longer feel her bottom. She wiggled her toes inside the mukluks to be sure they were still there, probably a little haunted by the memory of the chewed paw she had seen. Her hands were cold and she remembered that Mr. Marx's gloves were lined with lynx fur. She wondered if that one had pretty eyes too. Just then the sled beneath her slid over a stump and bounced hard.

"Blast him," she thought. "He hits those bumps on purpose, I bet."

Before she could commiserate further, the machine stopped and Mr. Marx's voice sounded above the machine noise.

"Well, if that wouldn't blow your tubes. Do you see what I see?"

"Man, he's still alive."

Pam scrambled off the sled.

"Mr. Marx, Mr. Marx. It's Wilma. See, she has those really white stripes. I know it's Wilma. She's trying to get out of the trap and she'll pull her foot off. Hurry. Hurry. Please hurry."

At the sight of the trappers, Wilma rolled on to her back in the familiar defensive bell position, raised her sharp white claws, bared her fangs and uttered a whistling, guttural, rolling sound. She shook the trapped foot wildly in a desperate bid for freedom. The effect was terrifying. No wonder trappers and Indians had called the animal a demon and a devil. Yet, what was more natural than an animal, freedom and life threatened, using all her devices to retain that freedom?

Tom could only mutter in stupefication, "Man, she is *furious!*"

Pam was more practical: "Please, please Mr. Marx, don't shoot her. Can't we take her alive and show her to the class. I'll take care of her. I know how, really, because the book told me lots of things. Please, please, can't we?"

"Cool your jets, chicken. I have no intention of shooting her; she's been too cooperative about letting me observe her, and I don't want to mess that up. But taking her home, now, that's a new brand of cat. You realize that there is more than one animal involved here, don't you? And what will your mother say? She'll probably get me fired if I let you bring home a biological specimen like this."

But he had to admit he was a little intrigued. He had never, in all his years of observation, seen newborn wolverine kits, and neither had many zoo keepers, because the wolverine seems to be inhibited by captivity. Pam's knowledge gained from the book she had read, and which he was ashamed he hadn't yet discovered, was impressive. Yet, he was extremely fearful they could not keep the kits alive.

The snarling inferno in the trap prodded him to action.

"Okay, Pam. Here goes… for trouble, and may bubble gum infest your beard forever more!"

"Oh good!" Pam pranced and bubbled and delighted. "Hurry, hurry, hurry before her foot freezes."

"Not so fast, young lady. Capturing wolverines is not that easy."

Tom had resumed his thinking processes. "Hey, I read an article in *Alaska Sportsman* by a guide named Branham. It took three pages for him to catch a wolverine. Used rubber tubed traps, and tackle and toggles and lots of crud. And he put him in a fuel drum."

"So maybe you've got an oil drum on you?" Mr. Marx sarcastically ventured.

"Sorry about that," replied Tom.

"Can't we put something over him?" queried Pam.

"I'm thinking, I'm thinking." And the teacher was struggling to recall details of a capture once made by Slim Moore, his longtime guide friend. The elusive thought came forward.

"Now I remember. Slim Moore used a canvas tarp. Then he caught the head and clamped the jaws shut with adhesive tape. Tom, get the canvas tarp out of the trap box. I almost wasn't going to bring that cover. Pam, find the first aid kit in that mess if you can."

When Tom returned dragging the heavy canvas in the snow behind him, William Marx took one upper edge and asked Tom to grasp the other.

"Now when I say go, we run forward and throw it over the critter. And drop it fast, because I'm going to try to surprise her."

"One, two, three—GO!"

Thereupon ensued the wildest, most unbelievable scene Pam could envision outside of hell. Snarling, enraged animal sounds layered with excited, screaming man sounds and all seemed concentrated in one mad heap of arms, legs and hurtling bodies.

"Hang on, Tom. Pam, quick, hold this side," and Pam dumbly obeyed.

"Now catch her head," Tom begged from his very prone position.

When Mr. Marx had ascertained in what general direction the heaving mass beneath the tarp was pointed, he calculated his next move. Diving over Tom, his broad hands encircled what he thought was a neck. Wilma let him know he had erred as she jerked a hind quarter loose with enormous strength.

"Woops," said Mr. Marx.

"Try again, Wild Bill Hickok," yelled Tom irreverently.

"Please hurry," pleaded Pam.

"I'll fix you, you wild female!" said Mr. Marx unmindful of his startled students. This time, his hands connected and the wolverine emitted another of her unearthly noises.

"I nominate you to put the tape around her mouth," volunteered Tom.

"How do you expect me to do that when I'm holding her?" asked Mr. Marx with just the faintest touch of irritation.

"But I'm holding the rest of her," wailed Tom.

And they slowly turned to Pam, who had edged back from the scene.

"Oh such babies," commented Pam with more confidence than she felt. She opened the first aid kit, rummaged for a large roll of white adhesive and began tearing a strip off the roll.

"How many feet of this do you want?" she asked acidly.

"About five," Tom retorted.

"Start with about twelve inches," Mr. Marx advised more calmly.

Pam ripped off what she thought was the correct length, then bit the edge and tore it off the roll. It didn't help that the cold was numbing her bare hands and fright was paralyzing the rest of her.

"Now listen carefully, Pam. I'm going to hold tight while you slowly remove the tarp from her face. Tom, you hold her body tight so she can't lunge at Pam."

Tom moved into tackle position and pushed the tarp close around the body. Struggling legs let him know his action was protested. The strength of the animal was unbelievable.

"Okay, I'm ready. What's taking you so long, Pam?"

"Shut up," said Pam.

Very carefully, she lifted the edge of the canvas and slowly drew it off of the animal's head. Despite the restricting action of Mr. Marx's hands, the animal still produced throaty sounds, and Pam hesitated every time one escaped. Finally, she threw the cloth way back over Mr. Marx's hands, and there for all the world to see was a white-fanged, beady-eyed, thoroughly alarmed wild animal. Pam sensed that the animal was really only fighting for survival, and suddenly she was afraid no more.

"Should I try now?" she asked absently.

"It's all yours, Miss Nightingale," said the ringleader.

Pam tried for first contact above the nose and landed. Then with assistance from Mr. Marx who was pressing the lower jaw upward, she swiftly swung the tape under and around the jaw, once again around, and the tape was expended.

"Maybe we should try another foot for good measure."

"That's a good suggestion," Pam agreed. "Why don't we let Tom mop up." Tom showed an amazing lack of willingness, and Pam finished up the taping operation, being careful not to cover the nose openings.

The two teenagers collapsed.

"Come back to the party you two. We're not done yet. We still have to tie this gal's front legs. Tom, would you like to have Pam do that for you too?"

"No sweat," said Tom. "Where's the rope?" He trotted off to the now thoroughly disarranged trap box and found a piece of nylon rope.

"I'll show you how Grandpa and I roped doggies on the North Dakota prairies," said Tom.

"Did your mother hold them down for you?" asked Pam.

But Tom surprised her by swiftly tying the front legs, maneuvering around the trap, then the hind legs, and slashing the excess rope with his belt knife. A whiff of wolverine scent rose from the knife.

"She should feel right at home with you," said Pam, holding her nose.

"Let's get that trap off, then figure out how we're going to get this thing back to the car," prodded Mr. Marx.

"Can't we put her in the trap box and sit on it?" queried Pam.

"I'm riding the sled home," said Tom.

"I wonder if Henry has an empty drum around his cabin," mused the teacher. "There's only one solution, kids. We'll release the trap and you kids can hold her down while I take the machine back to get some kind of cage. We're only a short run from the cabin now, and I'll be back in a hurry."

"Now let's get that trap off before her paw is permanently injured," said Mr. Marx. While he pressed hard on the steel spring, Pam gently lifted the paw free. Though there was some blood where the jaws of the trap had closed, the foot did not appear to be broken.

"Just in case, maybe we'd better cover her with the tarp while I'm gone."

"I don't like that *just in case*," said Pam testily.

Once more the tarp went over the animal and Tom moved to hold down one edge while Pam took up duty on the opposite side.

"Before I go, I'll get a fire going," offered Mr. Marx. With the help of a candy wrapper and Tom's lighter, a campfire was soon blazing close by the two animal custodians.

"I guess we have our work cut out for us, don't we Pam? I hope you don't break a leg on that trip back, Mr. Marx. My mother said

I should come home."

"Wait a minute," said Mr. Marx, and he was off through the trees.

"We will," said Pam tartly.

He returned with Pam's backpack and a thermos of consommé and handed it to Pam.

"You kids have a nice picnic while I'm gone."

"You forgot the marshmallows," suggested Tom.

He was answered with the roar of the snow machine, and then it was very silent.

A strange thing happened. With no third party to absorb their pointed jibes, they became unexpectedly aware of one another, and youthful embarrassment crept over them. Their eyes met briefly, then quickly averted.

Pam tried first: "Want a peanut butter and jelly sandwich?"

Tom recovered. "Thanks. No candlelight with our steak?"

Pam readjusted her bottom on a corner of the tarp, and placed her outstretched leg firmly along the edge; she ungloved her hands to pour some soup from the thermos, then reached over the lump between them to hand it to Tom. She followed with a frozen peanut butter sandwich.

"I prefer mine well done, but this will have to do," said Tom appreciatively. "Wonder why Wilma is so quiet," he puzzled. "Don't think I'll ask her. She's probably as tired as we are."

Pam chewed vigorously on the solid sandwich, then broke off a piece and tossed it under the tarp.

"Her mouth's taped shut, dope," advised Tom.

"It's not polite to eat in front of others," said Pam.

"You mean on top of others," Tom countered.

Silence enveloped them once more. Tom found he could lean against a tree trunk and still maintain his duty position; Pam stretched out her stomach along the side of the cloth and inelegantly rubbed her rear. Between them, the lump rested.

"Why do you suppose Alaska spruce are so scraggly?" Tom asked. "I remember last summer when I visited Grandpa in North Dakota, we went across the border to northern Minnesota and the pines were much fuller."

Pam replied with picturesque logic: "That's simple. Alaska spruce get so tired warming their trunks in the cold winter that they just have to rest in summer." And she snuggled her arms against her trunk to mimic the droopy, short-branched spruce.

"I never saw a lime green spruce before," he teased.

"I never saw an orange wolverine-holder, either."

"Touché, ma petite."

"Merci, mon cher."

Their eyes held.

"Here, put your hand inside my mitten," said Tom. "It's big enough for both of us."

She pulled off her moosehide glove and slid her hand into his warm glove. Her fingers awkwardly intertwined with his.

The moon must have descended very low because the shadows around them deepened. Pam shivered and eased closer to Tom, but there was that lumpy wolverine between them. Her head dropped to his shoulder. He rested his cheek against her furry cap. Through a break in the trees, he saw the Northern Lights come on stage now that their moon rival had passed on. The reds and purples danced with abandon and Tom felt a kinship. He saw that the fire was flickering low and knew Mr. Marx had been gone more than half an hour.

Pam was starting to doze when a deep, throaty roar shattered the night. Too late, Pam recognized that she had leaned on a wolverine paw. She screamed and clutched Tom. They saw the lump lurch forward. Tom dived for the tackle and Pam fell forward with his. They were so busy unscrambling they didn't see Mr. Marx walk through the bushes.

"Little activity here, I see. Sorry I took so long, kids. The machine threw a belt." He held up a 25-gallon oil drum. "Look what I got. It's one of Henry's water carriers, but it's about to become a wolverine cage. Let's go, Wilma."

"Don't just stand there—help me maneuver this baby into the drum." They lifted the cover, pushed the animal into the can, and snapped the lid.

"Help me carry it, Tom."

"Will she get enough air through that hole in the top?"

"For the short distance we're going—yes."

They opened the trap box and set the drum inside. Tom saw that

Mr. Marx had removed the other animals.

"Yes, I know," said Pam wearily. "I get to sit on the trap box this trip."

"I guess you know that wolverine can chew through steel traps and all kinds of cages," said Tom.

But the bantering had lost its bite. Tom put his arms around Pam's waist. Their eyes communicated.

"Let's both ride on the sled," decided Tom.

"Okay," said Pam.

Mr. Marx pretended ignorance and turned to his machine. He had seen and understood, but wondered what had caused such a change in forty-five minutes.

Down below, Wilma was wondering too.

Four

The exhausted threesome dragged themselves into the cabin of Henry TwoChiefs at 5:00 am. Henry had kept his promise and the Yukon stove was glowing red, chimney roaring. A stomach-stirring aroma of cooking food met their nostrils, and Tom could not resist an appreciative sniff over the pot atop the barrel stove.

"What is it, Henry?"

"Caribou. Onions. Roots. Medicine."

"Medicine!"

"He means herbs," Mr. Marx translated. "Don't worry, the only way you'll die is from overeating."

Without ceremony, Henry spooned stew onto the plastic plates and placed them on the square wood table. The guests needed no prodding. Henry pulled a handful of bread from the loaf his friend had brought and laid it on the bare table. The pile disappeared like cards from a dummy stack. They paused only long enough to move over when Henry joined them.

"Henry, my Mom doesn't cook breakfast like this. You should write a cookbook."

Henry TwoChiefs laughed with his friends.

When they had finished, Mr. Marx teetered back on his kitchen chair. "I think we'd better be thinking about that pay load in our trap box."

Henry's response was immediate. He arose, and began removing dishes from the table with agitation. Pam misunderstood and jumped up.

"For heaven's sake, I was planning to do them, Henry."

He answered abruptly: "Carcajou."

Nothing, but nothing had prepared Mr. Marx for this response from his Indian friend. "Henry! Not you! I can't believe it."

Tom finally comprehended. "He thinks the wolverine is an evil spirit?"

Mr. Marx answered, "I can't possible believe that our thoroughly modern Henry is superstitious. Do you mean, Henry, that you won't let us bring that wolverine into your cabin?

Henry lowered his eyes and shook his head vigorously.

"We'll, you're our host and I can't do anything you don't want. But Tom and Pam, you'd better zip up those zoot suits and make an inspection trip. Be careful. I took the tape off her jaw and paws."

Reluctantly, the tired teenagers moved to comply, but their hearts weren't in it. Their unenthusiastic departure did not prepare Mr. Marx for their animated return. Pam burst through the cabin door.

"Mr. Marx, she's acting funny. You better look."

It was the teacher's turn to become a reluctant inspector. He pulled on parka and gloves and plodded up the hill. Peering into the tilted barrel, he saw that Pam was right. The animal was panting heavily, her tongue hanging loosely. Her eyes were glazed and she emitted periodic guttural groans. Comprehension dawned.

"This is unbelievable! She's going to deliver."

"Deliver what?" queried Tom.

Pam fathomed faster and with the intuition of her kind moved into action. "Let's get her inside where it's warm or the babies will die."

The word "babies" did it, and Tom was goaded to movement. They clamped the lid back on the drum and carried it like a carton of eggs to the cabin. Henry silently moved to his bedroom corner, but curiosity overtook him. He watched with fascination as Pam pondered the building of a maternity ward.

"I know! Help me move the kitchen table to the corner. Now turn it over on its side and that will be one corner. What else can we use?"

"I saw a piece of plywood outside by the cache," suggested Tom.

"Get it quick." He and Mr. Marx headed for the door.

"And bring the tarp from the snow machine. We'll drape it over the top." When the makeshift den was completed, the maternity ward staff gently lowered the oil drum to the floor inside and opened the lid. Wilma shot out to a corner and fell into a now very familiar position. She snarled unappreciatively.

"She doesn't look very maternal to me," scorned Tom.

"You wouldn't be very good-natured if you'd been through all she has and then had to have a baby on top of it. Let's leave her alone for a while."

The occupants of the cabin busied themselves elsewhere, hard put to ignore the increasingly frequent birth sounds coming from the corner. Once Pam rose to throw a pile of rags into the corner, wondering what bedding a wolverine had in her den. Another worry crossed her mind.

"What if she won't nurse her kits when they're born?"

"I've been sitting here thinking the same thing," said Mr. Marx. "We'll have to be very careful not to touch the kits after she's dropped them because it might mean sudden nothing."

"What in the world can we use for a bottle?" wondered Pam.

Silently Henry uttered his first sentence since the drama had begun. "I have one in the cupboard."

Mr. Marx struggled to stay astride his tipped chair, then flipped forward. "You have what, Henry?"

Henry resolutely walked to the cupboard and from behind dusty fruit jars drew out a plastic baby bottle, complete with nipple. "I used it for moose calf once." He set the bottle firmly on the cupboard counter and walked back to his bed.

"Henry, you are full of little surprises today," muttered Mr. Marx.

Pam now pulled some babysitting knowledge to the front of her mind. Very precisely she found a pot, filled it with water from the drum behind the stove and placed it on the flat spot of the barrel stove recently vacated by Henry's stew. Then she washed the bottle and nipple with soap and placed it in the pot.

To the wolverine corner she addressed the next remark: "Now don't go too fast over there because it takes forever to boil water on these stoves."

Then she laughed when she realized that boiling water was part of every birth scene she had seen in old television movies. "Just like the movies," she pointed out to her audience.

"You're doing so well I hate to ask this. But what do you plan to put in the bottle?" asked Mr. Marx.

"Henry must have some canned milk around. Henry, say you do," she implored. Again Henry marched to the cupboard and handed her the needed item.

"I won't open this until I'm sure we need it. Thanks Henry. I wish I had Mr. Krott's book here."

"You had perfect memory when you were reciting on the trip up," Tom quipped.

"That was when I didn't need it. By the way, who gets the privilege of rubbing tummies and bottoms?"

"Let's not cross that bridge 'til we get to it. Wilma may not need any help. Wonder how many kits she'll have," wondered Mr. Marx.

He was answered by a long, decisive groan from the corner and they hurried to look through a corner of the tarp.

"Back up—don't let her see you," said Mr. Marx, stretching his neck further than anyone. "One more pain like that last one should do it."

"This is almost like when my dog had puppies," Tom compared.

And then it happened. The watchers struggled to see, yet remain unseen. Tom jumped to a chair and looked over the other two.

"It's here, it's here," said Pam. "Oh it's so wet, poor thing. Wilma's cleaning it just like our mother cat did." Then a horrible thought came to mind. "You don't think she would eat her babies do you?"

Mr. Marx had a worried look on his face. "I hope not. Let's watch."

Maybe because she was ready to resume more business at hand, Wilma nuzzled the kit aside and Pam was relieved to see it resting snugly in the clean rags. The second kit made its appearance and the licking process commenced. The kits needed no map to find the food supply and the wolverine acquiesced for some minutes. It was a short snack, though, because mother was back in the delivery business. She dropped another kit, then a fourth. The onlookers gazed in rapt attention as Wilma assumed full maternal responsibility.

"I think you should know that wolverine females will defend

their offspring jealously, sometimes against pretty rough odds. The males better not come around during the denning period, either," said Mr. Marx.

He continued, "Now what do we do? She'll try to devour us if we come near and she may not nurse her kits if we touch them. We can't leave them here with Henry, and we have to get back to Anchorage this afternoon. Now, will somebody give me a real sharp answer?"

After a thoughtful pause, Pam broke the silence. "What would happen if we put Wilma back in her den with two of the kits and took two with us? We could be real careful, maybe slide the babies without touching the other two."

Mr. Marx hesitated. "It seems mighty risky when the kits are so young. I wonder if Henry would let Wilma and two of the kits stay here for a few days, and then take them back to the den for us. Henry?"

Henry, long since resigned, understood perfectly. He nodded slowly up and down.

William Marx stared. "Pam and Tom, you just saw the bridging of a cultural gap in one nod of a head. Somewhere back when he was a boy, Henry was taught a simple fact. Superstition to us maybe, but fact to him. He just renounced that belief to do a friend a favor."

To Henry he said, "Thank you very much my friend."

Pam couldn't contain herself any longer. "You will let us take two of the kits home?" she begged.

"We can try. The odds are against you, but the scientist in me says it's worth a risk."

That was all Pam needed to begin a busy little housewife routine. She mixed formula—one ounce of already boiled water and one ounce of the sterile canned milk. She remembered that Mr. Krott had lost a kit in his book when he boiled the milk and she shivered. She poured the milk into the sterile bottle and screwed the nipple cap tightly.

"We can use my backpack for a nest!" She dumped the jumbled contents on the floor, then retrieved an old sweatshirt and crumpled it cozily in the bottom of the sack.

"The nursing staff is ready when you are, Doctor."

It was clear that Mr. Marx did not relish the task at hand. He put on his dark-rimmed glasses, and Pam couldn't resist a jibe.

"Now you'll be able to see what you're doing."

"Maybe it'd be better if I couldn't," he shot back. He surveyed the situation from the viewing window of the maternity ward. Wilma's brood was contentedly munching away as Wilma's busy tongue caressed them.

"I think we should all have an hour's nap before we tackle this problem."

A keyed Pam could only register disappointment. "I'm not a bit sleepy now and besides I can sleep all day tomorrow."

"Oh can you now? And who is going to feed those kits every three hours? I know one guy who's not."

Pam replied weakly, "I'll ask Mom to take one feeding and that will give me six hours of sleep."

Mr. Marx had already stretched his sleeping bag on the floor near the stove and Tom was following suit without the slightest hesitation.

"You can put your sleeping bag on Henry's bed, Pam. He's up for the day."

Pam eyed Henry who was complacently mulling his cup of coffee in a dilapidated armchair near the stove, then guardedly dragged her sleeping bag to the bed. She tossed it open on the caribou hide and a distinctly masculine odor of sweat reached her nose. "Oh well," she thought, "I'm not a bottle of Chanel myself right now." And she crawled in.

She knew she had slept when busy sounds within the room broke through the fog. With one eye, she could see Mr. Marx readdressing himself to the pressing problem in the corner.

He spoke with mock briskness. "Let's get with it crew. Remove two wolverine kits from wolverine mother." The he walked back to the kitchen chair and sat down.

Tom tried to help. "Man, there must be something we can use to scoop up those kits. Henry, where ya been? Come to the rescue, Man."

About that time, Mr. Marx's eyes fell on Henry's fishing gear winter stored in a corner. "Somehow, I see a fishing reel in this, but not quite."

Pam jumped. "That's it!" She untangled the rod in the corner. "See—we reel the kits away from her like this."

"With a hook in the tail, I suppose?" said Tom.

"No, we'll hook something soft to it… like my fuzzy hat. Then we just scoop the baby up and reel away."

"Have you ever tried to pull a baby kitten away from its mother while nursing? There's suction, Pam," said Mr. Marx.

"Then we could use a broom handle or something to nudge it first," replied Pam.

"And what do you think the mother will be doing while you two go fishing?" ridiculed Tom.

"We've handled one problem. Why don't you take care of that one?" suggested Mr. Marx.

"You could try diversion tactics—somebody could get her mad enough to come out fighting."

"You sure could, Tom," said Mr. Marx. "You just got elected wolverine-agitator for today."

"Why me?" wailed Tom.

Mr. Marx assembled the rod and reel and Pam stood ready with cap in one hand and broom in the other. They set a small hook into the knitted edge of the cap. It looked good.

"Mother will have a fit if I can't get that hook out," said Pam.

"She'll have more to worry her than that when you come home," added Mr. Marx.

He experimented by lowering the line gently into the maternity ward and slowly out again. "What'll you have—rainbow or grayling?" Wilma watched and commented with a low snarl.

"Keep it up, you're doing fine," yelled Tom.

"Get with it, Tom. You stay way over on that side and we'll get down near her. Jab the broom at her, do anything. Just get her growling!"

Tom did not expect such immediate reaction. He jabbed the broom in Wilma's face only once and that did it. Wilma played her part well, right down to the snarling, growling, whistling mad female that she was. And the nest robbers were not idle.

"Reel, reel, reel," squealed Pam.

The weight of the hat helped as he jerked the line out by hand. It settled near the kits. That was all Wilma needed. She leaped back to protect her offspring. Her paw swept at the hat and tore it from the hook.

"My mother will kill me," said Pam. "That hat cost $7.00."

"Why don't you make one out of wolverine hide," said Tom.

"Let's withdraw and reassess," said Mr. Marx.

"There's only one answer," said Tom. "We've got to throw something over her again. How about your parka, Mr. Marx?"

Ignoring the taunt, Mr. Marx said, "The tarp is too big and clumsy in this small place. What else?" He looked around the room. His eyes fell on the caribou hide. "Henry?" And suffering Henry once more played the perfect host.

This time Tom was ready. When he had taunted Wilma into a rage and brought her to his corner, he had the hide ready. Henry helped. The cover flew into the air and settled over Wilma. Tom leaped over the table and on to the writhing form. By now, he was an experienced wolverine holder.

"I'll give you one minute," said Tom to the nursery staff. Pam was already on her knees lifting a soft, furry, ivory-colored baby into a warm backpack. She followed with the second, being careful not to touch the other mewing kits.

Mr. Marx quickly replaced the plywood, but not before snatching up Pam's hat. Tom needed no instructions to remove himself from tackle position. He crawled back over the table and Henry lifted the caribou hide with broom handle. Wilma galloped back to her offspring. She sniffed suspiciously while the onlookers held their breaths. When she settled down to nurse and nuzzle the two remaining kits, Pam spoke sadly.

"She knows, doesn't she?" She turned to her new responsibility: two blind balls of fur hungrily nosing each other in the sweatshirt. The long waiting bottle, still warm, was passed to Pam.

"I'll warm the truck while you give them their first course," said Mr. Marx. Then you two can feed them all the way to Anchorage."

When he returned, Pam had managed to get a few drops of milk into the kits' mouths, but several more dribbled all over their little bodies. The nipple was too big for their tiny mouths, but by inserting her pinky finger into the jaw and prying it open she was able to occasionally insert the nipple. She alternated between the two, and was quite pleased with herself when they fell asleep after she softly massaged their small tummies and bottoms.

"We'll have to stop at a drug store the minute we get back to Anchorage," said Pam. "I wonder if they have smaller nipples. And we'll have to get two bottles so we can return Henry's moose bottle." She glanced gratefully at Henry who was smiling, very pleased with himself and everyone.

"Let's go."

"Wait, wait," and they watched while Pam unzipped her jump suit, gently pushed two tiny furry balls inside, and zipped up the suit. "Bring my backpack, Tom. I'm ready—what are we waiting for?" and she saw the group look at her almost admiringly.

Pam taught Tom how to give the next feeding in the car on the way home. She laughed when he clumsily attempted the massage routine, but refused to let him back out. "You're going to be helping me with a few of these feedings when we get home, in case you didn't know."

"Whose big idea was this anyway?" retorted Tom. But he smiled when he said it.

The warmth of the truck, the relaxing music from the car radio, and the sleeping kits between them produced pleasant euphoria. Mr. Marx smiled when he glanced sideways. Pam's head had fallen on Tom's shoulder and both were sound asleep.

Five

Word was buzzing through the school as early as fourth period. Mr. Marx had something simmering for seventh period. Pass the word. Ever since Pam Walker and Tom Lerner came back from the field trip, they were always whispering between periods, or going into Mr. Marx's office, or passing notes on the bus. Something was up, and the speculators pieced together their suspicions. The first Monday after they were back, Mr. Marx had Pam and Tom give a report to the class, and they told about the neat trip, seeing Wilma, freezing to death, and meeting Henry. But this morning Pam wasn't on the bus; her mother brought her to school late. They carried a box into Mr. Marx's office and the door went shut again.

The beginning bell rang for seventh period and Mr. Marx wasn't in the room yet. Tom Lerner was missing, too. Pam Walker sat at her desk looking like a fuse had just been lit. Then Mr. Marx and Tom walked in, and there was the box again. Bodies converged around Tom and Mr. Marx.

"Back to your seats, students. Or this box won't be opened today. Pam, why don't you come up here with Tom and display your biology specimens."

There was an appreciative murmur when Tom and Pam each raised a furry, ivory and brown colored ball for the class's inspection. The kits, now three weeks old, had just opened their eyes and were only beginning to show the markings of their mother—the side stripes and chin tufts. Their heads were already deep brown colored, and they had short black snouts and stumpy little tails. When Pam and

Tom placed them on the desk, they staggered on wobbly feet and mewed hungrily. They demonstrated how much their owners had taught them in three weeks by sucking zestfully at the bottles—the smaller nipples had been the solution.

"This is the funniest part of the feeding," said Pam, demonstrating how their tummies and bottoms were rubbed. As if to emphasize her point, a little stream of yellow spurted forth and with slight color. Pam emphasized that proper elimination was extremely important. She added that boiled milk contributed to constipation, so she boiled only the water, then added sterile canned milk.

"I also learned from a book I read that Vitamins A and B were very important. If they don't get enough A, they might go blind and have paralyzed hind legs; lack of Vitamin B produces skin trouble, paralysis and appetite loss. So they get a dropper full of that each day."

"We're not going to try to take them off the bottle for a while. But they'll get meat and cheese and eggs soon," said Tom.

"How often are they fed?" asked one of the students.

"Every three hours when we first brought them home, and was that a drag," explained Pam. But now it's every four hours, and if the house is quiet they sometimes skip a night feeding. It's just like having a new baby in the house, only worse because these are twins. But Tom helps after school."

"Are they boys or girls?" asked another student.

"Male and female," replied Mr. Marx. "And that's the first time in all my years of biology that I've had to make that determination. These are the first wolverine kits I've seen."

"What are their names?" came the inevitable question from a girl in the back of the room.

"So far A and B," said Tom. Pam and I have been fighting for a week about it."

"Why not Pam and Tom?" said a romantic girl in the first row.

"NEVER!" chorused Pam and Tom, and for once they agreed.

Pam said, "I think their names should begin with W since they are Wilma's children." And the class agreed.

"Walter and Wendy," came one suggestion.

"Willis and Wilda."

"Wilbur and Wilda."

"Warren and …."

"Wilberforce…"

"See, names with W are not easy," said Pam.

"I do like Wendy, but what goes with it?"

"Willy," said a student. "That's what we wanted to name Wilma, remember?"

"YES!" chorused the group. And Wendy and Willy were christened.

The class continued to inspect and discuss the small wonders while Tom related the hilarious capture and birth stories. They did not see Mr. Marx wander to the back of the room and slip out. If they had, they might have thought nothing of it, because he was a regular visitor to the drinking fountain right outside the door. But they did see him return. A burst of laughter followed.

"I would like to introduce you to an old friend in a new role," he explained. In his arms was the mounted wolverine that had graced his office all winter, previously decorated with a straw hat and flower in teeth. Now, the wolverine was wearing Pam's furry hat, slightly damaged, and in the paw, the conniving Mr. Marx had scotch-taped a baby bottle with nipple.

"We felt this would be a fitting memorial to a brave new mother in our midst, and from henceforth, it will be displayed in the showcase outside Science 5, a tribute for all the school to see."

"Mr. Marx, how could you," protested Pam. But she was laughing as hard as the rest of the class.

The bell rang. Mr. Marx put his hand on Pam's shoulder as they walked out of the room. "I've been on some pretty interesting field trips in my life, but I've got to admit ours was the wildest one yet!"

———

It was Mr. Marx who encouraged Pam and Tom to enter the school Science Fair. They would need to summarize their research using the contest reports which had won them the field trip, and in some way they must dramatize that fantastic day. Naturally Wendy and Willy would be on display. Since no photos had been taken,

Tom? decided to sketch some of the action scenes and he did not spare Pam in doing so. She especially protested when he depicted her in a lime green jump suit, nurse's cap and cape, the latter dramatically flowing in the arctic breeze. She was applying adhesive to an eager snout. Somehow it all came out scientifically, and Mr. Marx was as excited as they when the judges awarded them first prize in the Zoological Division of the local School Fair and first in the Greater Anchorage Science Fair. They lamented that they were ineligible for the grand prize, a trip to Detroit to the National Science Fair, because they were not yet senior high students. But the prospect of extending their experiment for next year's fair gave them an excuse to spend extra time together, which both enjoyed more than they cared to admit. They worked hard now to upgrade the exhibit for the regional fair.

It was the morning of the big day and Tom and Pam had been excused from regular classes. Wendy and Willy had been impossible. They much preferred to play-fight with each other rather than eat. Pam knew they must eat or they would be hungry before the judges had even reached their entry. Tom fed Willy while she brushed Wendy. Her exasperation led her mother to comment.

"I know the feeling, girl. I wonder how many times I've planned an afternoon out and the baby refused his bottle. But even though I knew he hadn't eaten a drop, he usually managed to burp on the shoulder of a good suit, and I spent the rest of the day smelling sour milk covered up with Woodhue No. 65."

With considerable unheeded advice, they finally drew up to the Alaska Methodist University fifteen minutes before deadline. They hastily arranged their display, wisely waiting until the last minute to put fresh straw on the cage floor.

"How about a Coke while we wait for the judges to give us first prize?" said Tom.

"I need more than one right now, but I'll settle for it anyway."

They threaded their way through tables in the student cafeteria to one in a far corner overlooking the sun-lit winter campus. Tom picked up Cokes at the cafeteria line and returned to the table. They sat opposite each other, both in an utter state of exhaustion. The emotional turmoil of preparing an exhibit and entering it on time had taken its toll and the two were silent for some time.

Pam was revived first. "I sure will miss Mr. Marx, won't you Tom? He's been a super teacher."

"Affirmative. Hey, maybe we can talk him into another trip to see Wilma this summer."

"Don't you have enough wolverines to worry about now? By the way, what are you going to do this summer? We're going Outside on a trip to Minnesota. Who's taking care of the animals?"

"Well, I was planning to work in my Dad's office most of the summer. I won't be able to."

"I wonder who… hey, how about the Anchorage Zoo? Let's see, they'll be one, two, three, FOUR months old then. They should be off the bottle and eating out of a saucer by then. How about it?"

"Sounds good to me. Or we could give them to Mr. Marx, ha!"

"We'll have to train them to a leash before then. Let's try around the end of April. We can walk along the bluff so they won't get tangled in bushes and trees."

Tom looked forward to any excuse for a walk with Pam and readily agreed. "Let's wander around the campus. Can't waste that sun. We've got a couple hours to kill before judging is finished."

They were waiting with a group of eager students when the chain barring entry to the exhibit section was lowered. With exaggerated nonchalance, they wandered back to their display.

Pam squealed, "*Oooohhh!*" Tom squeezed her hand.

"Sure like that shade of blue, don't you?"

The rest of the evening became a jumble of congratulations, picture taking, award ceremonies and even an interview with a local reporter. It pleased them when Mr. Marx put his arms around their shoulders and added his personal congratulations. The three shared a moment of emotion that they would remember nostalgically years later.

———— • ————

February slid into March and March into April, and though old-timers would scoff at the thought that winter was even remotely coming to an end, they were the first to note the snow level dropping and breakup conditions brought on by sunny days. Spring came sooner for those in the boonies who drove unpaved roads to work. They splashed through mudholes big enough to lose a car in, but onward and upward was the slogan. The dust that followed wasn't much to look forward to, either. An occasional moose wandered into town for a spree, then left when his presence was felt too keenly. Tom had even seen a small bear out on Point Woronzof while he was snaring snowshoe hare on his trapline. When bears wandered into town, newspaper reporters and mothers frenzied. Since the earthquake when half the point fell into Cook Inlet, Tom had seen fewer animals. They had probably decided enough was enough and wandered up to the safer reaches of the Chugach Mountains high above the city.

Tom and Pam had decided to experiment with leashes this Saturday morning. Tom was at Pam's door as promised. Mrs. Walker answered.

"Hi Tom. Come in. Pam's still trying to decide which pair of jeans to put on."

"Hi Mrs. Walker." Spying collars and leashes on the table, he said, "Hey, neat. Did you buy them for the cats?"

"I spent half of yesterday wandering through dime stores trying to find collars small enough for those dingbats. Even on those, you'll have to fasten it on the last notch."

"I'll try one on Willy. Hey, did you put the cage outside already?"

"Have you ever had a wolverine in your family room on a hot spring day, Tom?" asked Mrs. Walker.

"No, but you don't have to draw a picture," said Tom, sniffing, and remembering a certain sobering incident quite vividly.

Tom wandered out to the back porch where the kits inside their cage were busy chasing each other. Tom placed Willy on the warm porch to see what he would do. Pam watched from the doorway as the kit gingerly picked up each paw, then scrambled across the porch, put on his brakes, and balled over. Tom caught him and fastened the collar. Then he latched the chain to the ring on the collar and pranced around behind Willy. Willy decided this was a new toy. He rolled over on his back and snarled at the chain, snatching at it with all four paws. Pam had Wendy collared and leashed by now, and the two kits seemed entranced by this brand new state of affairs. They raced toward each other like two freight trains coming head on, collided like a couple hammy extras in a western fight scene, and the teenagers spent five minutes untangling chains.

When the foursome took to the open road, the animals were worse than puppies with their experimental nosing of every bush and rock, and they loved to run between legs. The teenagers soon learned they were being taken for a walk, not vice versa. They reached the end of the street and the bluff which overlooked Turnagain Arm. This was the earthquake slide area where some seventy homes went into the brink and it was now bulldozed over, a sandy, silent memory. Some patches of snow remained and there were still chunks of ice floating in the inlet. An oily smell reached their noses and Tom glanced towards the downtown port area to see if a tanker was unloading.

"Let's head out to my trapline," called Tom, as Willy pulled him forward.

"That's a long walk, Tom. I'm already beat with these kooks."

After a half mile of beach, the animals finally showed signs of lagging. Tom tied the leashes to a heavy piece of driftwood. They sat on a sandy bank which had been warmed and dried by the hot sun. Tom looked back at the Chugach Mountains guarding the city and noted the snowline had moved upward. It smelled like spring, and he had already seen pussy willows. He looked back at the Sleeping Lady across the Arm and wondered why this spring was different. He knew something had changed in him. Was this what they called growing up? Sometimes it hurt. Sometimes it didn't. Pleasant thoughts of Pam crept into mind and he turned to look at her.

"What?" she questioned.

"Nothing. Just thinking."

"About what?" she persisted.

"Oh everything. You and school and all."

"You mean leaving Romig? Umm. Especially Mr. Marx."

"Maybe he'll let us come back and visit once in a while."

"I thought you two planned to go sheep hunting together in August. Sure wish you guys would let me come along. I joined Rifle Club this year just so I could learn how to hunt… and I made pro-Marksman."

"Pam, for creep's sake, girls can't go where we're going. It's a 25-mile hike 5,000 feet up and besides we have to sleep overnight in the open in sleeping bags."

"Who says I can't?" retorted Pam, more interested in hunting than proprieties.

"Sheeeesh!" and Tom jumped up. He walked over, unhooked Willy and decided this walk should come to a withering halt. They headed home.

—•◦•—

Pam's Dad built a newer and stronger cage for Wendy and Willy. The new one had wire mesh around the inside because the animals had been gnawing on the wood slats of the old cage. Pam surmised they were teething and it reminded her of her baby brother when he crept under the table at about six months and blissfully gnawed away on a chair leg. Pam warned the younger members of her family to stay away from the sliding door at the top of the cage and to see that it was always kept locked. But curious little hands forget. She came home from school one night to find the door pushed back and the animals missing. She raced back into the house to determine first if the small boys had taken them inside to play. She was met with four "who me?" looks, then raced to the phone. She dialed Tom's number.

"Tom, they're gone. Can you come quick and help me find them?"

"What happened? Who let them out?" asked Tom, comprehending immediately.

"The boys left the cage door open and they're nowhere in sight. I'll start down towards the bluff. Meet me there, okay?"

"Okay."

Pam started down the street towards the Inlet, asking everyone if they'd seen the kits. She knocked on several doors, and the answer was the same. She saw Tom coming up the street from his direction just as she reached the bluff. They started down the sandy hill together.

"Let's look for tracks in the sand. Remember Wilma's five point track, only these will be smaller," decided Tom.

They veered back and forth from water to hill crest and were very discouraged.

"What does this look like to you?" asked Tom, bending over a very vague paw print.

Their eyes lifted in the direction the print pointed and Pam ran ahead a few feet.

"Here's another one, and this one is real clear. See, Tom, they start up the bank here. Let's follow."

The prints meandered up the hill sideways, backwards and up- wards, then finally turned back to Pam's street, following the backs of houses along the upper edge of the bluff. The boy and girl were so intent on following tracks they didn't see a figure waiting at the top watching them with interest. They were surprised to see a man in brown uniform, and then noted the Alaska Fish & Game patch on his shoulder.

"Understand you kids have lost something," he said pleasantly.

"How did you know?" puzzled Pam.

"One of your neighbors called," he answered. "We usually get a call when anything wild wanders into town. Having any luck?"

"The trail just led up here, but we won't be able to follow it on the paved street. We'll just have to think wolverine and check every hid- ing place on the way back," said Pam.

They looked up trees, not really expecting to find anything because they had never seen the animals climb one, but at this point they were being very thorough. They even looked in mailboxes along the street and searched the vacant lots with trees even more closely. No luck. When they reached Pam's house, she invited the man in for a cup of coffee and he accepted. Pam led him out to the sunny back porch and offered him the comfortable porch lounge chair.

"I don't think I should," he laughed oddly. His voice caused Pam to turn, curious.

"Why?"

"Come here."

Pam and Tom walked out to the porch. There, snuggled together blissfully asleep were the errant pets.

"I think I feel like Mom did when one of the boys got lost once.

She didn't know whether to spank them hard or hug them," said Pam with feeling. She lifted the animals and gently put them back in their cage.

"Now that I have a chair, I'd love that cup of coffee," laughed the officer.

Settled, he questioned Tom while Pam went off to get coffee.

"I know you kids have permission of the ADFG to keep these pets, but we're always interested from a research point of view in what's going on. Have any special plans?"

Pam handed him a cup of coffee. "We've been thinking about this Mr.... gosh, I don't even know your name."

"Sorry, I should have introduced myself before. I'm Bob Rausch."

"Mr. Rausch. Tom and I talked it over and we think we're going to put them in the Anchorage Zoo for the summer because I'm going Outside and Tom has to work in his Dad's office. He's checking with the folks at the Dimond H Ranch—that's where the new zoo will be."

"Sounds good to me. There aren't many wolverines in zoos Outside—did you know that?"

"They should be so lucky," joked Pam, still a little put out by the wanderings of the pair.

Several weeks later, Pam had even more doubts about wolverine parenthood. She and Tom were puzzling over homework inside the house when they heard an unearthly din arise outside. The backyard was alive with small boys, small girls, one St. Bernard dog, and two treed wolverines. The air was fetid with wolverine musk. Pam could not believe her eyes when she saw Willy far up the spruce tree clutching a limb as though he planned never to come down. Wendy was not so lucky and she clung to the trunk of the tree with all four paws, slipping back and scrambling up, glancing over her shoulder to check the upward progress of that wild tiger.

Bruno, the St. Bernard, pawed the tree noisily. It took great persuasion to push his massive hulk out the gate and lock it in front of his nose. He continued to voice his opinion from without.

"I thought one of those books we read said wolverines attacked dogs?" remembered Tom.

"Oh that was a husky dog that chased a full-grown wolverine, and she finally got tired and turned around and chased him. The dog came back to camp yiking with one wolverine chomping his rear," said Pam. "Now let's get these cats down." And she went to find a ladder.

School crescendoed to closing day. They went in to pack up report cards and cornered Mr. Marx in the science room after last bell. Now that the time had finally come, all the neat remarks had gone out of mind, and pure nostalgia took its place. Pam glanced around the room as though seeing it for the last time.

"This room has lots of memories for me," she tried.

"Me too," added Tom. And they were all suddenly without words.

Mr. Marx tried again. "You've been my top students; hope you learned something."

"That's questionable—for Tom at least," said Pam feebly.

"Keep up your work with the wolverines, and remember I'm around any time you need help. Tom, I'll probably see you in August."

"Thanks, Mr. Marx."

"Bye…" Mr. Marx suddenly got very busy with some books on his desk. Pam and Tom walked through the door.

They joined the crowd of ninth graders enroute to Spenard Lake for a water pistol fight. Later Pam sauntered up the driveway, sweatshirt and jeans dripping. Someone had tossed her in. She didn't mind. She felt better.

Tom's job would not start until a week later and the Walkers did not plan to start their long drive down the Alaska Highway until the end of June.

The two high schoolers were talking one day, feeling a complete letdown after the high-keyed pace of the last weeks of school.

"When do we turn the animals over to the zoo?" Tom asked.

"Dad said the lady said to bring them any time—just call ahead, that's all. We'll take the cage, too. Maybe we could do that tomorrow if Mom will drive us out."

She continued, "You know, I have an awful urge to get out of town. Do you suppose we could talk our folks into driving up to Caribou Creek? I keep wondering about Wilma and whether the kits lived."

"Hey, that sounds neat. You mention it to your Mom and I'll work on mine."

And there followed in the next days an artful study in parental persuasion.

Six

"Go slow, Mom. That turn-off should be just ahead," instructed Mary Lerner's son. "Everything looks so different in the summer time. Hope I can remember where that trail started."

"Besides, we were here in the dark last winter," added Pam.

"There's Milepost 100—won't be long now."

"Mr. Marx said we could always stop at the Alaska Communications site up ahead and ask a nice man named McKechni if we really get lost," said June Walker.

"There's Henry's cabin," spied Pam. "Stop on the turn-off right above it."

Mary Lerner moved slowly to a stop.

"Well kids, June and I agreed to get you kids to this trail, but we didn't offer to climb it for you. I'd like to stop down at Caribou Creek to visit with the Hitchcock's at their homestead. How long do you kids think it will take?"

"It's about a mile up there," said Tom. "But we want to watch for Wilma and that may take time. It's ten now and we have some sandwiches and pop so we'll probably eat lunch there. About one?"

"Okay, but don't panic if we're late."

"Mommmmm," protested Tom.

The two jean-clad, sweatshirted youngsters raced off the highway, down into a ditch and up to an opening in the trees. They pointed to the yellow BLM trail marker, then started up. Jean Walker and Mary Lerner watched them round a curve in the trail before starting the motor again.

"Oops forgot to tell them to watch out for bears," said Mary Lerner. And she laughed. "Can't you just hear Tom say '*Oh Mom!*' to that? Honestly, June, do we parents ever say the right thing at this age? But I think that doesn't bother me as much as trying to get information out of that son of mine. It's like priming a pump with a gallon of water to get a quart!"

"They're all different, I guess. I have one daughter who bubbles out everything, but Pam is something else again. I get the same feeling of frustration that you do with Tom. Do you think the higher the IQ, the quieter they get? I notice your Tom has been getting A's too."

"We can't complain about academic achievement, can we? That's why I've been going along with this wolverine bit. I think the kids really have something there. I'm hoping they don't goof off when it comes time for next year's Science Fair. Wouldn't it be something if they won the trip to Fort Worth?"

"I'd cheer louder than anyone. But did you ever stop to think about moving two wolverines to Texas? Holy Toledo, the Texans would never forgive us."

"Now that we've taken the size and oil statistics away from them, all they need is one of our wolverines!" And the ladies laughed for a mile over that one. Just above Caribou Creek, June slowed at a mailbox named 'Hitchcock', then turned slowly down the steep gravel side road.

Back on the trail, Tom and Pam were doing some reminiscing.

"Man, I'm sure glad I wasn't riding that sled over these bare muskeg hummocks," said Pam.

"Come on now, Pam. They feel like twelve inches of foam rubber under your feet. Why don't you let me tie the sled behind a jeep one of these days and run you up the hill? This trail is wide enough for a jeep, a little rough in spots maybe, how about it?"

"You weren't riding the sled, that's all I've gotta say brother."

As they moved on up, the highway sounds died away. In its place was a strange airy sound. To the city dweller, it would be a train passing somewhere in the distance; to the woodsman, it was the distant echo of a roaring stream.

"The birds are sure excited aren't they?" Pam noticed. "Listen to that one, Tom. Sounds like a soprano trilling, then dropping to alto."

"Hear that other one. He's really shook up. Sounds like he's saying 'Watch out! Watch out!'… in the key of G," he added.

They watched another small gray and black bird flit to a spruce top and twit-twit them vigorously. Up ahead, another bird sent a warning with three toots and lots of chatter.

Tom noted an area of black mud off the trail. "Why in the world do you suppose there are so many animal tracks in that mud? I see moose tracks all over the place. Do you suppose they stand in it to cool off like the pigs did back in North Dakota?"

Just then the morning sun went under a cloud and a few drops of rain fell. Pam pulled a plastic rain cap from the tote bag she carried.

"Afraid the rain will wreck that groovy hair style?" teased Tom. "It's kind of cute. Is it your own?"

"Yup, too busy buying wolverine food to afford a wig. Hey, do you think we'll see Wilma and her babies when we get to the lake?"

"Don't know. But we might see a bear," he said bending over a fresh bear dropping on the trail. "These look mighty fresh."

Pam was on her knees beside him, petrified. "Tom, that is one animal that absolutely scares me half to death. Moose don't bother me much, as long as there isn't a calf close by. But brownies send me right into orbit. Do you think we ought to whistle or something?"

"Okay, what'll you have—a little Simon and Garfunkel, or how about that march we played in the band?"

"Oh shut up."

They puffed up a steep rise in the trail and turned to look back at the summit. Both caught their breaths in surprise. Several miles below lay the icy blue-white Matanuska Glacier and behind it peaks of varying heights.

"It's beautiful," breathed Pam.

"Wonder what the name of that peak is?" asked Tom.

"We can look at my map," she answered, pulling a geological survey map from her bag. "Let's see—where's the sun? If we face the map this way, that must be Mt. Wickersham. Hey, I didn't realize that mountain was here. I did a report on that guy once."

"Get a load of that mountain name—Mount Sgt. Robinson," said

Tom pointing to the map. "Wonder who he was. Look it up for a report, Pam."

"Gosh that glacier looks pretty from here. Look how it winds around first left then right. Those hunks of dirt down in front look almost purple, don't they? Except for the dirty green tops. Wonder what grows in glacier silt. Look it up for a report, Tom."

Satisfied that they were even for the moment, they wandered on in silence for all of fifty yards. But their active minds could stand very little of that.

"How come we see all kinds of moose tracks, but never any wolverine tracks?" asked Pam.

"Because moose are 9,000 pounds heavier, stupid," helped Tom. Almost in answer to her question, Tom was bending over the trails. "Look here on this small rise—see the claw print—four marks forward and one little behind. At least I think I'm right—I don't think a bear print is this small. That's where to look for wolverine prints, I guess—on the upside of a hill where she has to dig in to get up."

"Or on the down side where she has to hold back to get down," said Pam sarcastically.

"Wish Mr. Marx was here to settle it," said Tom.

"Another thing I'd like to ask him is how come you don't see any wolverine droppings, and yet there are moose spore all over the place, and we just saw bear scat, too."

This time Tom wasn't so impatient. "Size again, I suppose, but I also wonder if it doesn't have something to do with their—well, I guess the word is fastidiousness or something. Remember how Wilma acted when we had her in that corner at Henry's? You guys probably didn't notice, but after you threw those rags in, I saw her do her job way back in the opposite corner and paw at the rags until she had it covered—just like a cat." They agreed to put that in their book of questions.

"Can't be too much farther to the lake. Mr. Marx said it was about a mile. I'm sure getting hot. That sun can stay under as far as I'm concerned, but it can't make up its mind today."

"Yea, first I'm hot, then I'm cold," said Pam pulling off the sweatshirt that covered a pink and orange-striped tank top beneath. Tom tried not to notice.

"I guess you could say Alaska weather is just like a girl, always unpredictable," replied Tom, but he couldn't help but eye Pam appreciatively.

"Sounds more like a boy, I'd say."

They reached the top of another ridge. Glancing round, Pam was first to spy the lake.

"There it is, Tom. Oh—isn't it gorgeous?" And it was. The dark green surface was glass still, mirroring mountain peaks in its depths. This caused Pam to look up at the original of the mirrored reflection and only then did she note that Sheep Mountain lay straight ahead. "Tom, look—way up at the top in those sandy crevasses before the green starts. Do you see those white dots?"

"Sheep! There must be 9,000 of them! Let's get those binoculars out of your bag."

The spots came closer and they were indeed sheep, all 9,000 of them.

"Wait 'til I tell Mr. Marx. Man, how can we miss in August?"

"Easy—you are no doubt aware that Sheep Mountain is in a game refuge?"

"Oh, we're not coming up here—we're going on the other side of the Matanuska."

Fascinated, they passed the glasses between them for a while.

Finally, Tom said, "Let's go down to the lake and find Wilma."

"You lead," said Pam.

They left the trail, and picked their way through blueberry bushes. "Bet these make good bear eating," teased Tom.

"Don't start that again," pleaded Pam. And at that very moment something caused her to stop dead, and look across the lake.

"Don't make a sound," she whispered, and pointed. Along the opposite shore, the heads of a moose and her calf swam silently for several yards; then they lifted themselves elegantly out of the water and over the steep bank. They shook themselves vigorously, then lifted their long legs clumsily as if the weight of the world were upon them, and quietly moved into cover.

"Weren't they absolutely darling?" said Pam, glad that they were on that side and she was on hers.

"Just darling," mimicked Tom.

They wandered closer to the lake, using a well-worn animal trail as the path of least resistance. They hadn't gone fifty more feet, when another sound alerted them. Halfway across the small lake they saw ripples, then another moose swimming silently across the lake. Neither dared to breathe as they watched the female turn to check out the suspicious sound that had sent her into the water. She snorted, and Tom wondered if it was a call to a calf or a dirty word to him. He looked anxiously at their side of the lake to see if a calf was following. None appeared. They watched the lady look back several times, ever alert, each time erecting her ears to catch sound. She looked right at them, but seemed not to see them.

"You would be wearing that wild top," complained Tom. "She'll probably come charging us at will like a bull."

"She's a lady," said Pam, as scared as he. Her heart was pounding fast and she was hoping fervently not to see a calf around. When the moose stopped mid-lake and seemed to turn to come back, her heart nearly stopped beating. But the animal changed her mind, and continued to the opposite bank where the other moose and calf had de-laked. But she wasn't in much of a hurry because she nibbled at the lily pads along the bank. This made Pam guess there wasn't a calf. Finally, the animal turned around, stared the onlookers full in the face, and lifted her hulking mass out of the water. It was then that they realized she was quite old, because she was much clumsier in her departure than the other animals had been. She shivered the water off her body, lethargically lifted each long leg and picked her way into the trees. But not before she gave them one last look and flick of her ears as if to say, "Have fun, kids, but don't stay too long—this is my territory." Later they saw her on the ridge above, only her face visible, ears standing straight up. When Tom saw her comical face peering at them he quipped, "There's the party crasher again. She acts like she's waiting for us to leave." Her presence was enough to deter Pam and Tom from walking closer to the end of the lake shore where they estimated they had seen the den site the previous winter. They were amazed to find how little they could remember about the exact location. They decided to go back up the ridge, find a good observation point and just wait.

They parked on a grassy spot above the lake and flopped exhausted by the scare of the previous moments. Almost simultaneously, they thought of food. Pam pulled two sandwiches from her tote bag and threw one at Tom.

"I did a little better than peanut butter this time. That's a real hamburger I hope you notice. Should still be warm because I wrapped it in two layers of foil."

"You're getting closer to steak each time. When can we come here again?" And Tom chomped away with appreciation. Another show was staging on the lake below. First Pam saw the V in the water, and squinted to see what was at the apex. The bird moved forward, gurgling nervously.

"What kind of duck is that, Tom? I never saw a reddish one like that before."

"Must be a Merganser. No, wait a minute, she's not big enough. Must be a Grebe. She's trying to divert our attention. Probably has a nest around somewhere."

Pam tossed a can of pop to Tom and flipped the top of hers open. "Sure have seen lots of flowers I don't know the names of today. Maybe I should impress Mr. Marx by taking them home and waxing them. Then if we get a quick call for biological specimens I won't have to raid Mom's greenhouse."

"We can do that on the way home," said Tom, nervously moving closer to Pam.

Tom shyly put his arm around her shoulder and she nestled closer to him. Tenderly, awkwardly their lips met, and the imprint of a first kiss was recorded forever. Engrossed with their private world, it took some time for the busy chattering to penetrate. When a parka squirrel skittered by their heads and scolded them briefly, they burst out laughing.

"Always a kibitzer in the crowd," breathed Tom.

But after months of hiding their feelings behind flirtatious jibes, they suddenly felt uncomfortably exposed. They were relieved when a splash in the lake reminded them that they had a wolverine to watch, and both were thankful to be back on safer, more comfortable turf.

"Did Mr. Marx tell you about the rough time he and Henry had getting Wilma back here last winter?"

"I never did hear all the story. What happened?"

"Henry let her stay about two weeks, then the stink got so bad he just had to get rid of her. But before he did, he left the cabin one day to hitchhike up to Sheep Mountain Lodge to pick up some supplies. When he came back, Wilma was out of the pen—oh, he made a better one out of plywood, because I guess he needed his table—and you should have seen the mess. She was all over the place—got into his cupboards and opened cans like they were going out of style. She even threw cooking pots off the counter and tore his bed apart. I can see why he was psyched out. I'll bet he's right back to thinking she was a devil carcajou."

Tom continued, "He fixed her though. He tied her outside until he was through cleaning the mess. The next day Mr. Marx came up to check his trapline and Henry was kinda definite about taking her back. They put her in the barrel again, and when they opened it up near the site here, Wilma shot out. She was so scared she forgot her kits for a minute. Then she turned around, jumped up on her hind feet and swirled her tail. Henry and Mr. Marx took the kits down to the den and shook them out of the barrel. They weren't even back up here when Wilma was sniffing around the door of the den."

"Gosh, I wonder how the babies did. Hope the change from a warm room to that steaming sauna didn't give them tuberculosis," said Pam.

"Toss me the binoculars and I'll have a look around down there," said Tom.

"Maybe we've been too noisy. Let's whisper from now on," and her voice dropped.

"Don't see a sign," said Tom. "Why don't you watch for a while and I'll take a nap. This sun is making me sleepy."

"Some scientist! Go ahead, be a party pooper. I might not wake you when I see her."

But Tom had already rolled over in the warm grass.

It was a full hour later when he struggled awake, Pam shaking and shushing him at the same time.

"I just saw something move down there—it was brown and the right size." She was moving the binoculars slowly right then left. Suddenly the glasses stopped moving and went down. She pointed to a spot at the end of the lake. The glasses went up. "Tom, she's there. I see her in front of the den and the kits are horsing around just like Wendy and Willy. They're trying to nurse but she's pushing them away. Oops, she's up and sniffing... sure glad there's no wind today."

The glasses came down and she asked Tom, "Where are we anyway? I mean if there was a wind would we be downwind?"

Tom calculated that the wind might most likely come off the mountain or from the glacier, but that would put them neither down nor upwind, but right across. "Crosswind," he quipped. "How about letting me have a look?" and she handed him the glasses reluctantly.

It was Tom who saw Wilma leave the den site and move up towards the ridge beyond the lake. "There she goes. Wonder if she's going hunting. Let's follow her, Pam."

Pam, remembering the moose and calf, was not so enthusiastic, but Tom coaxed and she consented. She was a little put out when she got a wet foot tramping through the marshy muskeg at the end of the lake. Tom led the way up the slope to the top of the ridge. They were surprised to see a large stream rushing between high gorges far below.

"That must be Caribou Creek. I didn't know it was so close," exclaimed Pam.

"I don't see Wilma, do you?" said Tom. "And I'm not about to climb those canyon walls."

"Let's give up, Tom. You know what a time we had following Wendy and Willy."

They decided to give up, which, although they'd never know it, was a very wise decision. For Wilma had some very ambitious plans.

She headed in the direction of Sheep Mountain, and settled down to a steady lope. She had many miles to go before she would find her prey. She knew there were young lambs high on those slopes and she knew she must go to them. She stopped at a small stream and lapped thirstily. Then she hurried on. Several miles later, she began her ascent, galloping through alders, spruce, and ground cover spread across the lower slope. The vegetation thinned and she became more wary. Sometimes, if it was necessary, the ewes wandered down to the lower vegetation, but more often they grazed on the rocky crags above. She would be patient and wait. She reared occasionally and inspected the air with her nose. Then she stopped. The hair on her spine bristled. She became intensely alert. She moved parallel to the new scant for a distance. Finally, she knew the time had come. She turned abruptly and sped to the target. She came upon her prey, a lamb with ewe, and took in the scene cautiously. She circled. The ewe noticed nothing. Wilma moved in stealthily. Instantly, the ewe bleated an alarm and moved to protect her lamb. Wilma sprang to the neck of the frantic lamb and buried her sharp teeth with a snap. The animal was dead immediately. The ewe disappeared up the mountain in total panic. Like all beasts of prey, Wilma hunted first because she was hungry. But not merely because of hunger. It was simply her nature to hunt as it was to sleep. And now she addressed herself to the meal. With her forelegs she braced herself and pulled at the head. When she had removed the skin, she crushed the skull and scooped out the soft brains. She moved on to the heart and liver and when her appetite was sated, she began to cache sections of meat. She dug a hole in the sandy slope and deposited a haunch. At one point, she scurried back to timberline and carried a leg into the trunk of a cottonwood tree. Chores completed, she backed up to the remaining meat, and marked it as only she knew how. Grasping a large haunch in her jaws, she started the long journey home to her kits.

Pam, blissfully unaware of Wilma's expedition, picked flowers on the homeward trail. She started with white Labrador Tea and purple Fireweed and then found a patch of yellow swamp Roses intermingled with purple Lupin and Monkshood.

"Know what a guy from Palmer told me about Monkshood?" asked Tom. "He says the farmers have to be real careful there's none in the pasture when they turn out the cows because it's poison."

"Yeah, we have some tame stuff at home, and Mom tells the little kids to stay away from it. I think it's the beans that are dangerous."

Further down, Tom added Alaska Cotton and Mountain Laurel to

Pam's collection. They found Dogwood and the pink flowers of the Low Bush Cranberry. There was purple wild Daisy and varieties they could not identify.

"Aren't you glad there's no poison ivy in Alaska?" said Pam.

They sat on the hillside beside the trail to rest. Pam rolled over on her stomach and spied the tiny Twin Flower trailing its way under a tree.

"Oh, here's my favorite." She picked the flower, double pink bells on a single stem and showed it to Tom. "Have you noticed that this vine puts down a root almost every place you see the twin flowers? And it smells heavenly," she said, sniffing.

After a brief rest, they raced down the hill and were almost at the bottom when Tom stopped. He picked a single Bluebell and handed it to Pam.

"You said it was your favorite," he explained. And he kissed her lips lightly.

Her eyes answered.

They raced down to the paved highway, crossed it and found a perching position high overlooking the glacier. It looked as magnificent as they felt.

Seven

"Kay has been after me for a couple years to drop in at her home-stead," said June.

"I'm curious—where did you meet her?" asked Mary Lerner.

"Oh, I took a course at Community College one winter, and she was my instructor. We're both interested in writing, and conversation got around to the homestead eventually. She's had quite a life out here. You'll like her!"

"How long have they had this place?"

"You won't believe it, but she and Ben came out here in August of '43 when she was about six months pregnant—and all they had was bare ground to welcome them."

"Good grief, she didn't have her baby all by herself in the woods, did she?"

"Not quite, but listen to this. The first night they were here, Ben put up a tent frame, he was a pretty good carpenter, and they got as many of their belongings under cover as they could. Then it rained, and I mean a downpour. Kay said the water was flowing under the tent like nothing Noah ever saw. But do you know—before Kay had her baby on November 21—Ben had dug a basement, dug a well, installed a pump, cut logs and brought them in with the dog team—oh yes, I forgot to tell you they brought their dogs with them. Ben raised the logs with a kind of tackle and pulley contraption, and let the dogs pull it. *And* he put a roof on the 24 x 24 cabin. Think we could ever get our husbands to move that fast?"

"I can't even get mine to put a washer in a faucet without an Act of Congress," answered Mary. "But get to the point—what about the baby?"

"Well, Ben took Kay out to the main road, that's where we just turned off, and this road was just a trail through the woods then. He took her out by dog team because they parked their car up there during the winter. Then he took her to Palmer to the hospital to have the baby. She stayed in town until December 10 of that winter."

"Don't tell me she brought a tiny baby back to a cabin?"

"Kay had me howling with that story. She tells about the first three days at home when she had to walk on bare floor joists because Ben was just laying the floor. Can't you see that picture—baby in arm, bottle in another, trying to walk across a room on joists!"

She continued, "That didn't phase Kay. Ben shot a moose and that was their meat supply for the winter. She'd managed to pick cranberries and blueberries before snowfall and that helped. Then they had a small tragedy. They'd brought along three goats for milk, and guess where they bought them—on Spenard Road in Anchorage. That was farm country then. Ben had built a shed for them, but the snow was so deep and there was just no browse. Feed was too expensive to buy, so they had to butcher their goats."

"Thank God for canned milk. I never heard of the stuff 'til I came to Alaska," said Mary Lerner. "Now I'm as bad as the old timers. I set a can of it on the table when I serve coffee, mostly for shock value, I suppose."

They were still meandering through the giant trees. "You notice this looks like a virgin stand of timber? I'll let Kay tell you *that* story. It's as hairy as the rest," said June. "That must be the homestead around the bend," said June, sighting a log building. And it was. They pulled off the road and parked. Kay Hitchcock came out of one of the larger buildings and walked towards them.

"June, you finally made it. Come on in," said Kay.

"Kay, this is my good friend, Mary Lerner. Mary, Kay Hitchcock."

The two greeted each other and Mary said, "I expected to find a weather-beaten, hardened old lady after what June's been telling me about homesteading. You look mighty normal to me."

Kay's eyes twinkled. There was immediate warmth in the response.

What Mary saw was a lady in her fifties, possibly late forties, gray-black hair, medium height, and what is generally called pleasantly round. But it was the soft, bubbling, but precisely grammatical speech that caught and held the listener. "Who ever heard of an English teacher homesteading?" thought Mary.

Kay led them into the main cabin. "What finally got you here?"

June answered, "We just let our kids off at Mile 103. They're climbing that trail in the interest of science. Remember I told you about those wolverines they are raising."

Kay answered, "Yes, I found that very interesting. I think I've seen a wolverine only once in all my years on the homestead, and that was at night in the headlights of my car."

She moved to the stove, and Mary noticed it was conveniently propane fired.

"I've just this summer moved back into this main cabin and I'm doing a bit of remodeling," she explained. Mary's eyes couldn't help but wander to the floor.

"June told me about the bare floor joists and your new baby," she explained. Kay laughed.

"These walls could tell a few stories. Some day I hope to set it all down in a book, but that's some day," answered Kay.

Coffee smell reached their noses, and Kay moved to serve it.

"Kay, I got up to the part about the goats passing out of the scene that first winter," said June. "Why don't you tell Mary more about it?"

They carried their cups over to comfortable old armchairs and settled into them.

"I think the biggest worry I had after that was Ben was subject to the draft. You see, we had left the CAA, that's Civil Aeronautics Authority, the old name for the Federal Aviation Authority, which was a sensitive position during wartime and Ben was deferred. So we decided to get the suspense over with, and Ben went down to Palmer, and I hate to admit this, but I was quite relieved when he was rejected for health reasons."

She continued. "That spring, I started my garden with a hand plow, oh about 60 by 100 feet. It's cooler here than in Palmer, but I was able to grow potatoes, turnips, lettuce, carrots and peas. See that area out by the river," she said pointed through the window. "The river has cut away the bank now, but in those days, I was able to grow my garden there."

"How much land do you have, Kay? The usual 100 acres?" asked Mary.

"No, about 85. We have three quarters of a mile along the creek now but we started on much less. You see, a man named Ed Ueeck had a trapper's cabin and cache out here, and in those days you just didn't consider overfiling on anyone like that, even if there wasn't a thing in writing. A few years later, though, Ed gave up his trap line and told Ben to go ahead and file. So our land starts way back there where the Matanuska River and Caribou Creek come together."

"How in the world does a person make a living on a homestead?" asked Mary. "They tell everyone nowadays to have $20,000 in the bank before they start."

"About all we had was determination. We were so poor, oh my, we were poor. So about 1944, until almost 1947, we tried our hand at gold mining. And I can tell you that is one way not to get rich. Especially with the problems we had. You see, Caribou Creek is a pretty fast river."

June replied, "Yes, I noticed that and I've also noticed it sometimes runs more muddy than usual. Why is that Kay?"

"Take a look at your map sometime, June. You'll notice that a great number of creeks drain into Caribou way back in the Talkeetna Mountains. There's lots of mud and sand at that level, not the usual trees and muskeg, and it washes into the feeder streams every time it rains. You notice the water is brown muddy, not gray muddy. Glacier silt is gray, and the Matanuska gets a lot of that."

"You were mentioning about gold mining, Kay," prodded June.

"Yes. In 1944 we moved way upstream to begin operations. And that was a story. You notice that Caribou Creek is bordered by canyon walls upstream? There's a trail along the upper ridge now, part way that is, but we fought our way through thick underbrush six miles up. During one of those years, I forget when, Ben built a small shack on a ledge just above the river. And we built our sluice box down on the water. But those canyon walls were just impossible. Every time it rained, the river rose fast and we had to remove the sluice box. Ask any miner how much he could get done under those conditions."

She continued, "But we did get occasional shows of gold. There's no question, that's mineral country up there, a lot of sand-precious stuff like jasper and agate. It's really rock hound country too, and there are fossils to be found also. But don't try to make a living at it," she added, wryly.

June noticed the sun had come out after a brief sprinkle of rain. "Let's take our chairs outside and talk," she suggested.

"I have some lawn chairs in the shed," answered Kay.

The ladies perched themselves on the banks overlooking the sand bars of Caribou Creek and far off to the left they could see bits of white glacier through tree tops.

"This is the lowest I've ever seen the creek in all these years," said Kay. "Even the stream from which we usually get our drinking water has dried up this year. You probably saw the trough near the road when you drove in. For the first time, I've had to carry water from town. But I can tell you there was no shortage of water a couple times," she laughed, remember that first week in a tent.

"Is that a kind of saw back there?" asked Mary, pointed back in the trees.

"Yes, our son, Jimmy is carrying on Ben's work. You see, after we learned mining was not profitable, Ben thought and thought, trying to devise a way to make a living without leaving the homestead. It was then that he conceived the idea of building pre-fabricated cabins. He managed to get a Bell saw mill which would cut legs an even six inches, flat on three sides, leaving the fourth side round. He was an ingenious carpenter, in fact an all-round Mr. Fixit, but I think the most imaginative thing he ever did was to invent a notcher. You know how logs must be notched at the corners, in fact, when you're building a cabin, this is the most time-consuming part. I mean, making the logs fit together perfectly. Well, Ben rigged up a device which would notch the logs. Before long, he was getting orders from all over. He would prepare all the materials before hand, even numbering the logs in the order they were to go up and of course notching and fitting everything perfectly—all this before we ever went to the cabin site. Little Nels and Ben and I would camp out in a tent while he was building the cabin.

"Kay, how in the world did you do it?" asked June.

"Maybe you have to be just a little crazy," laughed Kay. "But that wasn't all that happened in 1947. I look back now and I can truly say that 1947 was the blackest year of all. We had a great deal of snow that year and as usual, the road into our homestead was blocked. Ben kept the car up on the highway, and by the way, that was only being built when we moved up here in '43. We had to go into Palmer for supplies one day, so Ben walked up to the road to start the car—it was always frozen in those days. Some way, in trying to coax the engine to start, he cut off a finger in the fan. However, he never knew, because he was in a state of shock, and he managed to get up to the ACS station up there, it was still the CAA then." She pointed across the river to the communication tower. "The manager drove him to Palmer. But Ben sure left a trail of blood behind him."

"I guess the one thing that would worry me most about homesteading is trying to get to a doctor in an emergency," said June.

"I think maybe I must have had similar thoughts that winter," answered Kay. "About that time I thought I was pregnant but things just didn't seem to be going right. I didn't know it then but it was a tubal pregnancy and I know now that I was close to death one night. Ben walked to the CAA station and they radioed Dr. Haynes in Palmer. The doctor's car was frozen solid, but he got word to the Road Commission, bless those wonderful souls, and they came over to thaw him out and get him as far as our driveway. He walked into the homestead, took one look at me and said I belonged in a hospital. So Ben hitched up the dog team and they took me to the Doctor's car. Doc Haynes drove me to the Palmer Hospital. I know they saved my life. And I think there are hundreds of stories like this here in Alaska. You helped your neighbor when he needed it because it was simply part of being Alaskan."

"I certainly agree that 1947 was not your year," added Mary.

Kay smiled. "Oh, there was more. That was the year of the fire, also."

"Oh no!" exclaimed Mary.

"That also happened to be the year that Congress had decided to cut out firefighting funds for Alaska and the Bureau of Land Management was absolutely out of money. It all started one morning when we walked up to the mailbox. I happened to glance up at the ridge you saw back there when you turned in. I saw a tiny fire line of smoke. Jimmy went up to look at it."

"Jimmy?" queried Mary.

"Oh, I forgot to tell you, he's my son by a first marriage—he had come to live with us then." Jimmy came back and said the fire was already growing rapidly and heading towards us. There wasn't a thing we could do because the BLM couldn't help us and the neighbors wouldn't."

"What?" said Mary, startled.

Kay paused, hesitating. "I'll explain later."

"By early morning the fire was coming down the slope in our general direction. I don't remember why, but Ben wasn't home at the time, so I sent Jimmy up to the CAA station to try to find him by phone. It was two days before Ben returned and by then, the fire had developed a front one-half mile wide. In the frenzy of preparing to leave, I did a foolish thing. I put all our chickens in a crate and tried to carry them across to the other side of Caribou Creek. But the crate was so heavy I couldn't hold it high enough and every last chicken drowned. We ate lots of chicken that week. But to get back to the fire, there's one BLM man I'll never forget. Risking his job, because there were no funds left for firefighting, he came out and helped us anyway. We dug a fire line along the edge of our property. The men worked all night and finally finished early the next morning. When we awoke the next morning, a miracle had happened. The rains came. And when we went up to check our fire line, we saw the fire had come right up to it and stopped. It could have topped, of course, but the rains stopped that."

It was a while before the listeners spoke. The narrative been absorbing.

Finally, June spoke. "After that, it had to be uphill. You couldn't much further down."

"And it was all uphill," said Kay Hitchcock. "Ben continued his cabin business, and he also started making sleds. Did you know that he built all of Earl Norris' sleds for the dog races in Anchorage? He's made lots of sleds for former champions." And she referred to the annual World Championship Sled Dog races held during Fur Rendezvous in Anchorage.

June prodded, "Kay, tell Mary about your little venture into politics. Especially about the Alaska Party."

"I guess to tell that I'd have to go back a bit. The story of statehood would fill a book alone, but briefly, there were in Alaska at that time two points of view—that of people like Senator Ernest Gruening, who was active promoting the cause of statehood and others like Ben who tended to be more conservative and weren't quite what you'd call enthusiastic about Alaska's becoming a state. I use that word 'conservative' with qualifications because Ben's idea in starting a new party was to gather together people who did not hold to firm party lines either right or left, but more in the middle. You know Alaska had then and still has an enormous number of people who call themselves Independent. And believe me, they are. But to go back still further, and this is really very funny. It will answer your questions about no one to help us put out the fire too; Ben was actually accused of being a Communist during the war. You know we were all very pro-Russian then because she was supposed to be our ally. But the strange thing is, Ben never really trusted the Russians, and I think that was a very common feeling in Alaska. I wonder if it has anything to do with our Russian history or the fact that Siberia is just across the Strait from us. Anyway, Ben was such an individualist; he didn't care what anybody thought, so we got the *Daily Worker* delivered to our mailbox. Well, all he wanted was information on what the Russians were up to but you can imagine what kind of a stir that caused along the mail route. When the thinking turned against Russia along about 1945, he refused to stop taking the paper and that of course made him a Communist. But to get back to his politicking. He didn't really become active until about 1957, just before statehood became official. There was an organizational meeting scheduled the last week in December for the purpose of forming the Alaska Party—a group of the Independents I mentioned earlier.

"He ran as a candidate for the office of Delegate to the Constitutional

Convention which was scheduled to be held in Fairbanks, in anticipation of statehood ratification… that's as a delegate from the Palmer-Talkeetna area."

Kay sat back in her chair, and gazed over the creek, her eyes suddenly sad. "But Ben died just after Christmas that year." She paused, then continued, "I think now of that month before he died, and it takes on, oh a kind of spiritual feeling. Almost as though Ben knew he was going to die. It's strange, but that month was so perfect. The boys and Jimmy's family were home for Christmas and it was such a joyous time…"

Almost apologetically, she pulled herself back to the story. "I made the usual wifely gesture by filing in Ben's place. I didn't do one bit of campaigning because about that time I moved to College and went back to the University of Alaska to get my degree in Education. And do you know, I got quite a reasonable number of votes. I think it was a final tribute to Ben, a real Alaskan if there ever was one."

Kay stood up. "Enough of my life history. Let's have lunch. I have some caribou sausage that makes a good sandwich. And how about a piece of last year's blueberry pie—I mean the blueberries are from last year."

Later, the ladies wandered through the woods and Kay showed them orchids near the water. There were several Lady's Slippers, and the tiny white one looking so much like a Dutch shoe; there were also spiked orchids and Lady's Tresses. "I've heard so much about Alaska orchids, but this is the first I've ever seen," exclaimed June. "They were probably right under my nose all the time."

Kay answered. "You have to know the right time of year, like June, and their favorite spots."

They wandered back to the homesite, and Kay explained each of the buildings.

"I forgot to tell you that Jimmy continued on with his Dad's work, and that's another story. But you've had enough."

"Come on Kay, don't quit now," said June.

"At the time he died, Ben had already taken down payment from the Girl Scouts to build them a cabin. I was really in a predicament because we had used the money to buy some of the supplies and there wasn't a way in the world for me to return that money. So Jimmy came to my rescue, and when spring came, he trucked the pre-cut lumber to the site and built the cabin. Thank heavens, he had worked with Ben before and knew about as much as Ben. Anyway, he's still at it!"

"Kay, I think your story is fabulous. You certainly should write a book. How in the world do you manage to teach and run a homestead at the same time?"

"I go into Anchorage twice a week for summer courses. In the winter, though, I move into town and go on a fuller schedule. Commuting isn't easy by dogsled these days," she teased.

"Well, feel welcome to stay at our house any time you're in," said Mary, "but don't expect me to come up with any wild tales like yours."

"That reminds me… when Ben and I were first married, we tented one summer on Point Woronzof in order to fish for dog food!"

"That does it!" exclaimed Mary.

"Then, later, we built a cabin at what was the end of KFQD Road, Northern Lights Boulevard now. Our cabin was still there even after the earthquake, but when Jimmy and I went back for a nostalgic look this summer, it was gone. I think the man to whom we sold it moved it away. I must learn where it went."

Mary replied, "My son, Tom, will be very interested in that story. He traps rabbits on Point Woronzof."

June said, "That reminds me—we promised to pick up the kids after lunch. Kay, I can't thank you enough. Promise you'll stay at our house soon."

The friends parted. Mary Lerner mentally marveled at the unusual woman she had just met.

Eight

June Walker was furious.

"Did you ever hear of anything so stupid? Here I spend weeks getting this pack ready for a sheep hunt, then walk off without my jacket."

It was August, and they were at the foot of the BLM trail which led to Wilma's den and sheep country. Her daughter answered. "Now we'll have to wait until Dad gets here with the trailer and we'll be late getting back to the mountains before dark."

"Let's drive to Kay's cabin and see if she has an extra. It's only three miles from here."

They reached the Hitchcock cabin and were relieved to see Kay come out the door, spatula in hand. "Hello! We're just having breakfast, come on in. Will you have a cup of coffee?"

"Thanks no, Kay. I just had a cup from my thermos."

Pam and June followed Kay into the cabin where a Yukon stove roared warmly. Kay flipped the eggs in the frying pan atop the barrel stove, then introduced her son, Jimmy.

"Where's the rest of the family? You certainly don't plan to go sheep hunting alone, do you?"

"They're coming later with the trailer, and plan to park up the creek. Pam and I started earlier in order to get back to sheep country before dark. We want to be close to them before the season opens at midnight."

"But I thought Pam and her Dad were going hunting," said Kay.

"So did I. But that old war injury flared up again, and he can't walk for any distance. So guess who got hooked."

"I just couldn't let Tom and Mr. Marx beat me," said Pam. "They were so mean about not letting me go with them."

"You may have some different ideas when you come back," said Jimmy. "Sheep hunting is dangerous even for men."

"Well, I've made the first mistake of the day… forgot my jacket. You wouldn't have one to loan me would you, Kay?"

"How will this do?" asked Kay, pulling a blue denim jacket off a nail in the bedroom adjoining the living room.

"Do you think it will be warm enough? You know how they've already had snow in Fairbanks. I've heard of August frosts in Alaska, but no snow."

"Here. You can wear this wool sweater under it. That jacket is good for walking through bushes. Doesn't catch. Wool is good for warmth."

"You're a doll, Kay. I was so mad at myself." She turned to Jimmy. "Now, can I pick your brains, Jimmy?" She sat on the sofa beside him and spread a map across their knees. "This is where we're going—up this BLM trail to the lake and ridge, then we're following Caribou Creek around to Dan Creek. Now, will we have trouble crossing this creek?"

"No problem—it's just a small creek. Be sure you swing left away from Caribou though, because it's pretty marshy near the creek."

"Have you heard whether there are any sheep back here on Fortress Ridge?" asked June. "We saw them in June but they may be gone now."

"McKechnie flew over last week and saw lots of ewes and lambs, some legal rams." He was referring to the ACS site manager.

"Good. We'll head for the Fortress Ridge then. How far do you think it is? About three or four miles?"

"No, by the time you wander up and down around those ridges, it'll be more like seven or eight."

"Ugh. These 25-pound packs are murder. And Pam has to carry the gun. We weighed it on the bathroom scale and it weighs eleven pounds."

Pam spoke. "Can you imagine how awful it'd be to have forty pounds on our backs? That's what Tom and Mr. Marx are carrying. But they're staying longer than us, and they eat more."

"We've got enough food for three days—lots of dried stuff, peaches, raisins, fruit bars, beef sticks, stuff like that. And water. We'll need that when we get above timber line." June stood up and put on the sweater and jacket Kay had given her.

"That looks better on you than me," said Kay who was a few inches shorter than June.

"Good. I'd like to impress the bears." She walked down the narrow hall to the door. "Bye Jimmy. I enjoyed meeting you. And thanks Kay. I'll return these when you come to town next week."

"I forgot to ask you, will Mr. Marx be crossing the Matanuska from our property?" asked Kay.

"No, they've gone further upstream, and plan to take a ferry or bridge across, I forget which. They're going to hunt near the South Fork of the Matanuska."

"I'm relieved. That river is treacherous. And you said they planned to cross in a small boat."

"I think I talked them out of that when I told them what you thought about the idea!"

Pam and June got into the car and waved to Kay. "Wish us luck," called June.

"Hope you get a sheep. See you next week."

June and Pam drove back to the beginning of the trail, parked the car in the gravel pit out of sight, and clumsily backed into the straps of their packs. Pam picked up the rifle and they were on their way up the trail.

"Thank heavens it's a cloudy day. I'd never make it with this heavy pack in a hot sun."

"It's your turn to take the gun," teased Pam. They had been on the trail ten minutes.

"Oh no you don't, gal. I'm carrying the Primus stove and fuel because you had to carry the gun, remember?"

"Just thought I'd try."

When they reached Wilma territory, they stopped at a ridge

and looked down at the lake. All was serene. Pam glanced towards the slope where she and Tom had picnicked and remembered her happiness.

Her mother interrupted. "Don't you think this would be a good spot to try a practice shot, Pam? I'd hate to get eight miles back and find something wrong with the rifle."

"But we might spook the sheep."

"They're miles away, yet."

Pam removed the cover from the gun, carefully loaded, and then from a prone position, zeroed in. She fired and was a fraction off target.

"Good girl."

"Nuts. I was an inch off."

"I figure it's good when I'm six inches off," said her mother. "That's good enough to hit a sheep."

"Not good enough in rifle competition," answered Pam.

"Let's go, Pam."

They hiked slowly to the end of the swamp buggy trail, then followed an animal path towards the river through alder, muskeg and berry bushes.

"Jimmy said to bear left away from the river here," said June. It was quite a few days later before she learned that he had meant way left around the ridge that now loomed before them. Several miles later, they came into the open above Caribou Creek. To the left and far, far below them the creek came out of canyon walls and moved downstream towards them. At the bend in the creek they saw water falling from the top of the mountain to the creek.

"My map says that's Dan Creek, but that sure doesn't sound like the little creek Jimmy said we'd have no trouble crossing," said June Walker. "What do you think, Pam?"

Pam looked at the map. "The map shows Dan Creek coming into Caribou at that bend. Must be. But look, Mom. We can't get around up there. There's a big slide."

"Wonder if that's always been there or if the earthquake broke away that bank? Now what do we do? We can walk way back around that ridge or go down to the creek floor and cross the

Caribou down there at that narrow point, then go back up to Fortress Ridge from there. What do you think?"

"We could toss a coin," said Pam.

"Seriously, Pam, how about it?"

"Let's go." That was their second mistake.

They reached the edge of the canyon and peered over the edge at a dry creek bed which stair-stepped down the mountainside. They began to pick their way slowly down the bed, around boulders, dead tree trunks and shale slides. June soon found herself descending on the seat of her pants.

When the bed dropped too steeply, they detoured to the side and lowered themselves between alder branches, passing the gun between them.

"If it's this hard going down, I hate to think of getting up again. Sure hope we can find another way out of this canyon," gasped June.

"I see the bottom, Mom." They walked into a level area of alder trees. Pam collapsed to the ground, propped against her pack. June sat down and eased out of her straps.

"Whew. Let's split a can of pop."

"I hope you see the fresh bear signs over there," noted Pam.

"Right now I wouldn't move even for a bear," said June. "Open that pop, kid." June unscrewed the thermos top and thrust the cup toward Pam. Pam flipped open the pop and poured some into her mother's cup.

"I see now why Mr. Marx said to take along lots of energy food like sugar and protein," said June.

It was fifteen minutes before they felt the urge to move on. Just ahead they found Caribou Creek. The river seemed much wider and swifter than it had looked from above. They moved along sand bars until they reached the narrow point they had picked as a crossing point. June's heart skipped, but Pam was already removing her shoes. She pulled off her boots and rolled up her pants legs. They jammed their footgear into their packs and June picked up the gun. Pam waded in and slowly they moved across the rocky bottom of the swirling stream. June had to look high to the opposite bank because the water made her dizzy. She tripped on a rock, but caught her balance. Her heart pounded faster, her foot numbed. Thoughts of falling and a soaking sleeping bag whirled through her mind. Pam scrambled up the bank ahead of her and turned to urge her mother on.

"Come on, Mom. Just a few more steps."

June reached the bank emotionally exhausted. "I've got to put my boots on and warm my feet before we cross again, Pam." June rubbed her numb toes, then slipped on the warm socks and boots. Pam had worn an old pair of tennis shoes for the crossing and sat looking at her mother sympathetically.

"Must be age," said Mrs. Walker, noting that Pam didn't seem to be suffering as much as she.

"Those rocks don't hurt my feet with these shoes on. Let's cross again or I'll be as cold as you," urged Pam.

They hiked several hundred yards up the sand bar in order to make the next crossing. Once more they forded the stream. This time it was wider and faster because the canyon was narrower above. Pam stepped into a hole and felt her pants legs get wet. She was carrying the gun this time and it threw her off balance. By the time she reached the opposite bank, she was chattering. They broke speed records getting socks and boots on this time.

"We've got to find another way out of this place. I can't cross that stream again," shivered June Walker.

"Let's start looking," said Pam.

They walked around the bend in the river and stared up at the slope that had been hidden from their view back on the mountain top. They were dismayed to find it steep and shale-covered. Defiantly, Pam scrambled up. June followed. They picked their way up, first through muskeg, then more and more shale. They found footing as long as the shale chips were deep, but they soon reached a spot where there was only rock outcropping.

"I can't get across there. I have to come down," called Pam.

"If you can't make it, I sure can't," said her mother.

They slid down the hillside on their backsides, then paused to decide the next move. The wind howled ominously through the canyon and drops of rain fell.

It was already 5:00 in the afternoon and it would be dark at 9:00. "Let's go through those woods to the waterfall," suggested Mrs. Walker.

They moved into the tall spruce and cottonwood and felt suddenly comforted because the wind was stopped by the hill they had just tried to climb. The moss was soft under foot. Dan Creek belied its name as it fell from a height of fifty feet through solid rock, then tumbled among boulders and fallen trees to its meeting with Caribou Creek. The water was clear, unlike the muddy Caribou.

"We can fill our canteens here," said Pam.

"I still can't figure out what Jimmy meant when he said this was just a small creek. I'll bet he's never been down here on the canyon floor."

"Only dopes like us come down here," said Pam.

"Well, now what do we do?" asked Mrs. Walker. She looked at the bank opposite the creek and her eyes followed it upward. She mentally plotted an upward course and it looked promising.

"Pam, do you see how that moss zig-zags across there? If we could follow it up, we might get to the top."

"I can't even see the top from here," said Pam. "Please Mom, let's go back and try that first one."

"I just can't figure how we're going to get across shale, Pam. This looks like it has more moss. Come on, let's give it a try… please?"

"It just looks too steep, but I'll try… I guess," said Pam. She sat down against her pack and pulled the straps to each shoulder. Her mother did the same and led the way. The first step was six feet above them. Mrs. Walker tugged at an alder branch hanging over the creek and with a grunt hoisted herself and pack up the rise. Pam handed the gun to her, then pulled herself up. The trail they had seen from the ground proved to be only ten feet in length. It was again necessary to hoist themselves another five feet. When they had both pulled themselves to this next level, they began to realize what was ahead of them. They must climb what looked like an almost perpendicular grade. So far there had been occasional spruce trees and moss over the shale. June glanced at the creek far below and resolved not to look down again until she reached the top. They reached the third ledge and rested. Pam was ready to try for the fourth long before June was. June saw her disappear behind a huge spruce high above. She called out, "How does it look up there? Will we be able to make it over the top?"

Pam's faint answer came back. "Come on Mom, it's better up here."

At this point something happened to June. She had the sensation of complete immobility and exhaustion. She realized a tautness in the pit of her stomach, then nausea. She knew now that fear had taken over. So this was what mountain climbers faced. How in the world could they scale cliffs with only a piece of steel and rope between them and the rocks below. She waited almost five minutes. Pam called from above.

"Hurry up Mom. What's the matter?"

"I'm resting," lied June. "Let me pass the gun to you," she called. "Then it won't be so hard to get up."

After what seemed an age, Pam's face peered over the cliff. June felt bits of shale hit her face.

"Mom," pleaded Pam, "please come on… you make me scared when you're scared."

"I'm sorry, Pam, I'll just have to admit I'm chicken."

She handed the gun up, stretching to her utmost until the tip of Pam's finger touched the muzzle of the gun. One more push and Pam had it in her grasp.

"Now come on," urged Pam.

"Pam, could I tie a rope to my pack and have you pull that up too? I just don't think I can pull myself up with this pack on my back."

"Mom!" At this point Pam was near tears, partially in fear and partially in exasperation.

June fumbled through her pack and found the nylon rope. She tied one end to the aluminum frame of her backpack and tossed the coiled end up to Pam. Pam pulled the pack up while June pushed from below.

"Now *come on*, Mom," pleaded Pam.

June closed her eyes and with all the will power at her command, dug her feet into the moss and pulled herself to the ledge. She kept going up the mossy slope until she got around the spruce tree where Pam had stashed her pack and the gun. What she saw behind the tree overwhelmed her. Far above them was the top of the ridge, but in order to get there, they had first to cross not only shale slides but bare rock as well. She looked down at the creek far below and felt sick again.

"Pam, we simply cannot make it to the top. Let's go down."

"Never. It's ten times harder going down than it is to get to the top. You can stay if you want, but I'm going up." And with that she commenced the climb across bare rock and shale. Bits of loose shale clattered behind her. Mrs. Walker closed her eyes in complete panic. Pam started slipping back and lunged for a small spruce, sprawling almost prone against the mountainside. She dug in a toe and turned around, crying.

"Mom, let's go down."

June had already begun to do just that. She tied the rope to the gun and let it slide out of sight until the rope stopped pulling. Then she tied her rope to the other end and lowered it. It stopped before the rope ran out. Before she could panic further, she turned around and slid inch by inch backwards on her stomach. She felt the small thermos in her jacket pocket slip out and heard it bounce from rock to rock and crash far below. Her foot touched the ledge where her pack and gun lay. She hoisted the pack to her back. Pam was right behind her. They lowered the gun to the next level, then moved on down. Pam slid past her, grabbed an alder branch and jumped the last six feet to the creek bank. She grabbed the gun as June lowered it on the rope. Neither uttered a sound. It was as if each was in a race to defy the danger they had so intimately experienced minutes before. June jumped the last six feet and scrambled across the rocks in the creek. She fell exhausted beside Pam. Her heart was pounding and Pam was half crying

"I have never been so terrified in my entire life," gasped June.

"I can't even breathe," said Pam. "Mom, what can we do now? We have to get to those sheep tonight."

"Sheep? You're talking about sheep at a time like this? All I want to do is get out of here." Then she knew she had frightened Pam even more and a small glimmer of common sense returned.

"We're going back to the woods we came through just before this stream and make camp for the night. It's already seven."

"Do you mean it took us two hours to climb that small way?"

"Small way? Did you look down when you were up there? I thought we were halfway to heaven!"

"Now we'll never get a sheep," wailed Pam.

"Come on, girl. We're making camp."

She led Pam to a flat dry spot some yards back from the waterfall. Pam's eyes spotted a pile of old tin cans.

"Look, this was somebody's camp. Here's a rusty coffee can and these are old mess kits. And here's an old tarp."

"I'll be darned. I thought we were 9,000 miles from civilization."

"Look! There's an old tobacco tin nailed to that tree."

"They must have used it for a target."

Pam investigated the square tin. "It has paper inside it."

"What is it?"

Pam unfolded the sheet and read: "To Whom It May Concern: This writing is to declare the intentions of the undersigned parties to claim and record this location as a headquarters site under the territorial laws which govern such claims. Signed T.A. Goodrich and John N. Goff." The paper was dated May 10, 1949—over twenty years before.

"Now I'm really curious. I'd love to find those two men and ask them how they got here. Wonder if 1949 was a dry year, too, or maybe they came in on the ice and stayed all summer until it froze again. Wait a minute! Now I remember. Kay mentioned someone named Goodrich. He had some kind of gadget which he claimed would detect not only ore, but the size of the lode, a sort of super Geiger counter. I'll bet Goff was the ex-GI who worked with him. I'd still like to know how they got in here and if it was a high water year. Do you suppose that slide area was here then, or do you think the big earthquake caused that?"

"Hey, look at that pole nailed across those trees way up there. Bet that's where they hung their game."

"Here's the bottom of an oil drum—they must have cut it off for a stove base. We can use it to build our fire in. I'm so afraid to start a fire in this moss. It creeps under and before you know it the whole woods is on fire. That's what happened with the forest fire that started last week."

Their spirits lifted as they watched the fire flare. The smoke smelled good. They cleared ground under the trees for a sleeping place. Pam tied the nylon rope between two trees and Mrs. Walker stretched a plastic sheet from the rope to the ground.

"What a difference between this plastic ground cover and that heavy tarp they used. No wonder they didn't pack it out."

"Do you think this plastic would still be here after 20 years?" asked Pam.

"I don't know. Do you realize plastic has only been invented for a little over 20 years?" answered her mother.

Pam cut clothespins from the green wood and pinned the plastic to the clothesline. They gathered rocks from the creek and laid them across the end of the lean-to.

"Let's put my ground cloth on the other side and make a tent instead of using it on the ground."

"Are you still worrying about bears after all we've been through today?" asked Mrs. Walker.

"I'm scared of bears," said Pam in a small voice.

"I think you'll be sorry if you don't have that ground cloth under your sleeping bag. Remember there's permafrost not far below those soft spruce needles. Here, I know what we can do. Let's use Mr. Goodrich's heavy tarp for the other tent side. I'll use his old mess kits to bang together and scare bears."

"Perfect!," Pam agreed with enthusiasm.

They gathered leaves and spread them beneath the lean-to.

"Don't tell Tom or Mr. Marx we slept on leaves or they'll know we were below the timber line," said Pam.

"Mr. Marx and Tom can go to heck," said Mrs. Walker irreverently.

After they had spread their sleeping bags on the ground cloth, they concentrated on dinner. Mrs. Walker got out the tiny Primus stove, a bare 3 x 3 inches, and poured a few drops of fuel into the crevice beneath the orifice. She struck a match and watched the fuel blaze up for a minute. Then she opened the petcock and heard the hissing sound that meant the stove was functioning. Soon the yellow flame died and the blue flame burned like a blow torch. June opened her mess kit and poured water from her canteen into the small cooking pot. Within minutes the water was bubbling.

"Isn't that stove something? Mr. Marx said it was hotter than sin. That man at the sport shop who sold it to me was a mountain climber. Wonder why Americans didn't invent it first," she wondered, noting the Swedish manufacturer.

She prepared instant hot chocolate and coffee. Then she heated a can of stew. They ate and were quite pleased with themselves.

"I suppose you-know-who would have something to say about carrying canned stew instead of the dehydrated stuff, but I'll bet they wouldn't turn it down if they were here now," said June. She was pretty pleased with herself.

They washed dishes in Dan Creek.

"Some pressure in this water system," said Mrs. Walker wryly, nodding towards the waterfall upstream. "I'm thinking about Jimmy and his small creek. The end of the stream fell off. About fifty feet."

They returned to camp and Pam saw that the moss under the oil drum had ignited.

"Let's set the drum on those old coffee cans, Pam. Here, help me lift the stove with these old frying pans." They moved the smoldering fire to its new perch, then dug up the blackened moss and poured water on the hot spot. They went back to the stream and carried more water. Finally, the area stopped steaming.

"Let's walk out to Caribou Creek and see if any sheep have come down," suggested Pam. "Remember we saw those sheep droppings this morning."

Pam picked up the binoculars and they walked through the quiet woods. It was 8:30 and quite murky because of low cloud cover. They reached the big river and Pam shivered; the wind was still whistling through the canyon and raindrops spattered her face. They peered hopefully up the mountainside but the sheep were still far above Fortress Ridge, that elusive spot they had set out for so many hours ago.

"I don't know about you, but I'm going to bed," said Mrs. Walker. She started back to camp. Pam followed, dejectedly.

"Better load the gun and put it beside your bag," said Mrs. Walker.

"I thought you said we didn't have to worry about bears?" complained Pam.

"Oh that's in case a sheep comes over that slope during the night," laughed Mrs. Walker. "Put the gun in this, pardon the expression, game bag. It won't get wet." She handed Pam a plastic garbage bag.

Then she washed her face with a Wash-n-Dri, buttoned up her sweater, took off her boots and crawled into the mummy sleeping bag.

"Goodnight."

"Boy, that's the fastest I ever saw you get to bed," observed Pam.

"I suppose you plan to put your hair up in rollers?" said Mrs. Walker from somewhere inside the bag. She couldn't believe her eyes when she peaked out a few minutes later and Pam was carefully rolling each pig tail in a large plastic roller. It was half an hour later when Pam finally crawled inside her bag. Her mother noted she had tied a wool scarf over her face.

"My nose gets cold at night," explained Pam.

They drifted off to the sound of raindrops on the plastic roof.

Some time during the night, Mrs. Walker wakened long enough to feel aching muscles and wondered where the aspirin was. Next time, I'll remember a pencil flashlight she thought. Pam was out of sight in her sleeping bag. The woods were quiet save for the soft sound of the rain. She snuggled further into the bag.

Nine

When June opened her eyes again, it was daylight. The rain had stopped, but the sun was still somewhere beyond the ridge. "Probably shining on those damn sheep," she thought. She rolled over in the sleeping bag and peered out under the lean-to. Her eyes wandered lazily upward through the open spot in the tree to a sunny spot on the hillside above, stopped, and puzzled. She tried to sit up but the zippered bag stopped her. She tugged at the zipper and it relented.

"Pam."

No answer.

"Pam." Mrs. Walker punched the bag full of daughter.

"I'm sleeping."

"Look."

"You look."

"Where are the binoculars?" Pam bolted up not waiting to unzip the bag and flopped like a seal to her mother's viewpoint.

"They're in my jacket pocket. Why?"

June raised the glasses. "Yup. They're sheep. How far is it?"

"I know what you're thinking. If I shoot one from here it might roll right into camp." Pam was wide awake now. "Where's my jacket? Where are my shoes? Get the gun."

"I'm going with you, gal. This I can't believe."

"Where's my ammunition?"

"In your pack. Come on, let's go."

"Let's go up that way behind them, then come down from the top," whispered June, tracing the route with her fingers.

"That's what Mr. Marx said—you're always supposed to come down on them, otherwise they'll scoot over the top away from you."

They'd paid no particular attention to this small hill the day before because it seemed to lead nowhere; evidently there was something on the other side that they did not know. They crawled through loose shale for a distance, then moved to the left through moss to get behind the sheep. Near the top, they moved slowly and silently, and June now saw that this slope connected with Fortress Ridge several miles away. She looked down and saw Dan Creek waterfall and a sudden queasiness returned. But this time, it was different. Pam was cautiously kneeing her way up the mossy slope. When she reached the top of the ridge she peered over, then turned to June and excitedly motioned her on. June hurried up and looked over the top. Elation surged through her when she saw what Pam was pointing to. One hundred feet below them on a rocky ledge sat five sheep: a ram, two ewes, and two lambs. The ram and ewes rested on their haunches, enjoying the morning sun; the lambs frolicked a few feet away.

"Are the horns big enough, do you think that's a ¾ curl?" whispered Pam, hardly daring to move her lips.

"They're pointing forward, they look huge to me. Hurry up," said her mother in her barest whisper.

"I'm so scared my arms are shaking." Pam released the safety softly and rolled on to her stomach. She raised the rifle to her shoulder and sighted for what seemed like an eternity to her mother. Then June saw her finger slowly squeeze the trigger and thunder echoed through the mountains.

"I hit him! I hit him!" shrieked Pam, bounding up over the ridge. Chaos reigned below. The ewes and lambs bounded in four different directions, but their target had leaped into the air and rolled over the edge. Pam slid down the slope to see if the animal had stopped. She sighted him falling in the direction of their camp.

"Come on, we have to catch him!" she yelled.

"I'm coming, I'm coming!" her mother yelled.

The descent was a record. June caught up as Pam was bending over the ram.

"He's almost gone. See, here's the bullet hole. I got him through the shoulder."

June felt knees giving. "I'll go down to camp and get the salt and knives—and the game bags."

"The instruction sheet is in my backpack, in case I forget how to do this," said Pam. She noticed that the ram now lay still and was glad it hadn't taken long. While her mother was gone, she traced her finger around the curl of the horn and mentally counted the inches. Did they say that 46 inches was the Boone & Crocket record for Dall sheep? These looked huge, but Pam knew there were quite a few inches less than 46.

"I couldn't find the instruction sheet," said Mrs. Walker when she returned. She handed the boning knife to Pam.

"Nuts. I hope you remember some of the things Mr. Marx told us about cutting meat."

"I remember how to start—the Fish and Game man drew a picture on television the other night." June knelt beside the ram and moved its head to look at the horns. "Oh, you've already bled him," she said. "How did you make that cut?"

"I had a pocket knife in my jeans. Mr. Marx said it was real important to do that as soon as possible so the meat wouldn't be tainted. Be careful, don't mess his front, that won't come off if we mount the head."

The pair began their tedious work with a v-cut from the horns straight back along the neck, then down around the front. They took turns with the hack-saw when it came time to remove the horns from the hide section.

"Man, am I glad I sharpened these knives before I left home," said Pam, starting to skin the hide away from the flesh. "Now I see why this skinning knife is shaped this way." June spelled Pam when they sectioned the meat; she had helped her husband cut up a moose once and remembered a few steps.

"Man, this is the roughest part of shooting a sheep," said Pam.

"Oh is it now. Wait 'til we start hauling this stuff out of here. I don't even want to think about crossing that creek."

Hours later they completed their work. The meat was in plastic bags.

"We're supposed to put this meat in cheese cloth game bags, but I'll be darned if I'm doing to carry drippy meat all the way home," said June. "We'll put it in cloth and hang it when we get back to the trailer."

"I'm glad you brought plastic bags," said Pam. "I already look like something out of a horror movie." She lifted a bag of meat and put it down fast.

"Wow, this is heavy."

"We're supposed to tidy up after ourselves, but I sure hate to bury these bones when the animals could finish this up." She pulled the remains of the sheep under a spruce tree, then covered up the messy area with moss. "I think we're going to have to leave the hide, Pam, and just take the trophy section. We just can't carry meat and horns and hide."

"But, Mom, I wanted it for a rug in my room. Can't we just get it across the creek and leave it in a plastic bag—and maybe Tom and Mr. Marx will come back with me to pick it up?"

"You must be out of your head, child."

"Please?"

"It's your funeral. But you'd better salt it well. Let's get back to camp and salt this trophy section again. One thing, our packs will be two pounds lighter with the salt gone."

It was creek crossing time again and this time June's stomach was really churning. They had jammed as much meat as possible into their backpacks, but there just wasn't room for all of it, so they had tied the nylon rope to another plastic bag. The hide was wrapped securely inside another bag and the meat rested on it. They planned to cache the hide somewhere near the creek bed. The horns were propped securely atop Pam's sleeping bag. She looked very funny.

"You wade across first, Pam, and take this end of the rope with you. When I start across, help me pull this meat across. I'll try to hold the bag as high as I can. This water is a lot higher than yesterday from the rain."

They sat down and removed their footwear. Pam put on her tennis shoes again.

"Brrr. These tennis shoes are still wet from yesterday."

June stuffed her boots into her sleeping bag and hoped they'd stay put until she forded the stream. The wind was still making inhospitable sounds through the canyon and she shivered. Pam lifted her pack and wrapped the coil of rope around her hand. June helped her put her head through the straps of the gun so it rested on the top of her pack just in front of the horns.

"I wish you could see yourself," she chuckled.

She watched Pam pick her way across the swirling, muddy yellow water. The river seemed wider than yesterday. When Pam waded up the opposite bank, she stepped into the icy water herself. The heavier pack made balance precarious and the extra bag of meat made matters worse. She concentrated on watching Pam reel in the bag because she was feeling dizzy again. Inch by inch, the opposite sand bar came closer and June scrambled over the rocks when she neared the end. Pam pulled the heavy meat bag ashore. June's feet were numb, but she was surprised to see Pam crying.

"What's the matter?"

"My feet hurt so."

"I know sweetie. Mine were the same way yesterday. I can't figure out why they aren't as bad today. I think those wet shoes don't help you any. I'm going to put on my boots and warm my feet before we cross again." She sat down and rubbed her painful feet.

"Please, Mom, can't we just keep going and get across the next creek... then build a fire?"

"I think you should try to warm your feet before we try again, Pam."

"Please, let's just go, please."

"You must be really cold. Guess I have so much adrenaline pumping by now that it's acting like anti-freeze."

They walked up the sand bar to the next bend in the stream and June watched the water slam the canyon wall upstream, then angry at being thwarted, return wildly to the rocks near them. They stood gathering nerve once more.

"You go first, Pam, and we'll pull the bag across again."

Pam stepped into the fast water and hobbled across the rocky bottom. June followed, stumbling once in a hole. Pam was crying and in complete misery when they sat down on the beach.

"You'll be okay soon, sweetie. Get your warm socks on. I'm so relieved to be across that water. One degree colder and we could have walked on it. Hurry up, honey, let's walk so our feet get the circulation back."

"Mom, I can't even feel them."

"I thought you said they hurt?"

"Can't we start a fire?"

"No, it will take too long. Here, wear my dry tennis shoes." She fished them out of her pack. "Come on, move."

They followed the river downstream to a point they had marked the previous day with a Coke can on a branch, then turned inland to the mountain. They found their resting place of the previous day, but it took them fifteen minutes to locate the creek bed they had come down. Very fresh bear signs did not brighten their spirits. June peeled an orange and rested at the bottom of the creek bed while Pam pulled the plastic bag containing the hide up to a high cottonwood branch. She secured the end of the rope to a lower branch and cut off the rope.

"Just enough left to drag that bag of meat up the hillside," she added.

"This is going to be a rough climb, Pam. We'll just have to climb and rest and climb and rest until we make it to the top. Seems like two weeks ago that we came down that darn thing."

They followed the bed upward for fifty feet, then moved over to the moss for better footing. Pam moved ahead, then pulled up the gun and the game bag; they repeated the process over and over again. June blessed the alders because they gave her boosting ballast. In order to rest, they propped themselves in the upward crotch of a tree because they slope was too steeply graded to allow them to stop otherwise.

"Ouch," cried June. She had grabbed a raspberry bush to pull herself up. She removed a thorn, then detoured to the right. Pam was just above her. "Pam, pull the gun up, will you? What do you see up there?"

"I'll take a look." She disappeared.

A faint voice came back to June.

"Come—on--up. We're—at—the--top." Pam was using their method of calling out each word slowly. June felt herself reaching the exhaustion point again; her heart pounded relentlessly. She summoned one last spurt of energy and climbed to Pam. They flopped in a blueberry patch and viewed the falls and river below.

"Pam, we've got to have a picture of this; Dad will never believe it." She wearily maneuvered out of her straps and pulled the camera from a side pocket of the pack. The scene was recorded. They nibbled beef sticks and fruit bars and energy returned. It was four o'clock in the afternoon when they reached the end of the trail.

Back at the trailer, June Walker threw her arms around her husband's neck. "I've never been so happy to see anyone in my life," she said.

"I worried about you last night," said Mr. Walker. "I was afraid it was snowing back there."

"Last night was the least of our worries. We were snug as bugs. It's the rest of it…" and thereupon began the account, properly embellished every successful hunter's fashion.

Two days later, a truck drove into camp. Tom jumped out one side and Mr. Marx out the other. Pam saw they were much cleaner than she had been and she wondered where they had changed their clothes.

"Okay, start bragging. Suppose you got a Boone and Crocket trophy," said Pam.

"How did you do?" asked Mr. Marx.

The story was retold with greater embellishment and Pam got a promise of help in retrieving her hide. Then she showed Mr. Marx her set of horns.

"They only measure 36 inches but they look like 56 to me. What size are yours?"

Mr. Marx looked at Tom. Tom looked at Mr. Marx.

"Should we tell her?" asked Mr. Marx.

"You tell her. I can't," said Tom.

And there began a sad, sad tale of two hunters who got skunked.

Tom had shot a sheep, but he hadn't fallen; they tracked him for over four miles then gave up. By that time every sheep on the mountain was spooked, and they came home.

"I'm really sorry," said Pam. Her sorrow lasted all of one minute. "Why don't you join Rifle Club, Tom? They teach you how to shoot there."

Tom would hear variations on this theme more than once during the coming year.

Ten

"Hi Beautiful!"

Pam Walker whirled around intent on squelching some fresh young man with a withering look. When she saw it was Tom standing with a group of boys, the icy intent evaporated and she walked over to him.

"I'm so lost in this high school I feel like finding a hole and crawling in," she confided to Tom. "Don't you wish we were back at Romig?"

"From the scoop I've picked up, this first day is mild compared to what a couple guys have cooked up. Tim Brady tells me he heard a couple cats talking about us getting our names in the paper and they figure we deserve special attention in the thumbditty department."

"Gosh, Tom, do you think they'll do anything mean? Will it be as horrible as you always hear about seniors and sophomores?"

"We could always bring Willy and Wendy down as protection. Man, can't you see those seniors after we present them with a little Chanel No. W… there goes first bell, keep the faith!"

"See you later, Tom. If they find my body in a closet around here, bury me up on Caribou Creek!"

Somehow Pam fumbled and scrambled her way through first day at West High School and after the first week, she was amazed to find herself falling into a routine as uncomplicated as the past years at Romig. But one thing still bothered her, and she was constantly waiting for the second shoe to drop. She had heard wild tales of initiations in past years, made better in the retelling, and the threat related by Tom on the first day did nothing for her peace of mind.

She just wished they'd get it over with so she could walk down the hall without shivering every time she saw a senior. It was bad enough wearing the 'sophomore' tag demanded by custom.

During fifth period on Thursday Pam was finally starting to relax, and confided to Tom that maybe these initiation threats were just talk.

But after sixth period, the other shoe finally dropped.

She was racing to get to her next class before the bell when she saw what appeared to be a wall of upper classmen moving down the hall towards her. It was really only three seniors, but it looked like a wall. She tried to veer to the other side of the hall and slip through the cordon, but they were too quick. She received her ultimatum.

The rest of the school day was a blur and Pam couldn't find Tom fast enough after school. She yelled to him as they both raced to the bus, "Tom, it's awful, wait 'til you hear what we've got to do."

Their heads were together all the way home, and anguished groans escaped above the din of the bus crowd. It didn't help one bit when they poured out the story to Mrs. Walker; they expected a sympathetic ear, but she thought it all hilariously funny. They groaned over their preparation work that night, then in an unusual show of mutual concern, sat down and helped each other with homework.

An Assembly had been called for second period, a sort of "now-that-you're-all-settled-and-had-your-fun, next-week-will-be-serious-and-down-to-earth-won't-it?" type of warning. The principal had just finished his rousing remarks when a disturbance was noted at the rear door and everyone craned necks to see "what now?" A parade was in progress. It was led by a young lady wearing a placard around her neck, which informed the assembled students that she was one of a foursome of "Kool Kats." Trailing her on a leash was one curious wolverine named Wendy similarly emblazoned; next, a young man, also with sign, was followed by one very reluctant Willy. They were motioned to the center aisle by a smug senior class president and instructed to parade down the middle aisle, up the stage steps, over the stage, down the side steps and out the side aisle to the rear door. The red in Pam's cheeks far outshone the lettering on her sign. The auditorium crowd was in an uproar and the laughter was shared by teachers. When Pam reached the rear door and found both her mother and Mrs. Lerner laughing just as hard, it was too much. She handed the leash to Mrs. Walker and raced down the hall to the girl's lav to anguish alone. She anguished, but not alone. There were about twenty other sophomore girls sympathetically clucking over her. She did recover. After this baptism, nothing could ever again be too difficult in high school.

Through a little finagling, Pam and Tom had been able to get into the same science class. Needless to say, word of their scientific endeavors had preceded them, and they were happy to find their new teacher, Mr. Moore, not only sympathetic but ready to push them even further into research on the wolverine. They discovered that Mr. Marx had given Mr. Moore considerable information on their work thus far. They discussed with him how they might upgrade their project for next February's Science Fair.

Tom remarked, "We've read almost every available book on the wolverine now. I have this bibliography which some undergraduate at the University of Alaska compiled, and we've checked off every book that's available in Anchorage."

Glancing through the list, Mr. Moore noted, "What's this addendum to the list? I note you've scribbled initials next to each title."

Tom answered, "Oh those initials are for places where those periodicals are available. ADFG stands for Alaska Department of Fish and Game; AHL means Alaska Historical Library in Juneau; INF means U.S. Institute of Northern Forestry; BCF means U.S. Bureau of Commercial Fisheries and SJJC means Sheldon Jackson Junior College in Sitka. The reason we don't have any of those articles is because these officials are all way down in Juneau and you know the cost of an air ticket to that place."

Mr. Moore mused thoughtfully, "Some of these article titles seem very interesting. Do you suppose… I have a good friend in the library there. I wonder if she could contact these agencies and photocopy any of these articles for you?"

Pam joined the conversation, "Mom has a good friend who is the wife of a legislator and she goes to Juneau with her husband every January. Maybe she would look up the articles and send us copies."

"Good, Pam. Follow that through. Now do you have any other ideas for upgrading your project?"

Pam and Tom really hadn't given it much thought. They'd been too busy keeping their specimens fed and clean. Wendy and Willy had survived the summer at the zoo very nicely; in fact, they had been rather spoiled by all the attention.

Pam had an idea. "Do you think if we kept a daily log of their learning processes from now on it might add to information already available? I mean, when we did our first science fair project, they were only a few weeks old; we could summarize their progress for each month since that time, like we could tell when they first ate solid food, when they first climbed a tree, when they were trained to the leash and we can tell how they reacted to a dog."

Mr. Moore agreed, "Those are excellent ideas, Pam. Be sure to include that important first-month log, also, because knowledge of newborn kits is very rare. Then, you could follow through with a month by month log as you've suggested."

Through considerable arm-twisting, Pam was able to persuade her two younger sisters to give up their backyard playhouse in the interest of science. They covered the floor with insulation, then laid a piece of plywood over that, followed by a layer of straw which the two had purchased at a local feed and seed store. They watched from the dutch door of the playhouse.

"Do you think they'll be too cold in the middle of winter?" wondered Pam.

"How could they, Pam? You know it goes to 45 below zero up near Caribou Creek, and it sure never gets that cold here in Anchorage. I remember one time when it went to 30 below zero here, but that's only once. It barely went below zero last winter. But if it does get real cold, we can take them inside until the cold snap is over."

"Oh can we now? Suppose you take them inside your house. I haven't found the cologne that will cover up wolverine smell yet."

"That makes me think of something funny Grandpa back in North

Dakota said. He said farming was an honorable profession, but one thing that always bothered him when he was a boy was that he could never get that barn smell off him when he went to school. But his trouble was that he had to milk ten cows at 4:00 am, then rush into the house, change his clothes and walk a mile to school."

Pam asked, "Couldn't he shower before he took off?"

"Are you kidding? They had an outdoor toilet, and the well was a block from the house. He and his brothers rigged up a shower for the summertime by putting a barrel up on a platform and filling it mostly with cold water from the well, then adding a tea kettle full of hot water to take the chill off. Boy did they wash fast before the water ran out. Then, they walked a mile into town for their dates smelling like pure, fresh well water."

"Okay, I'll quit complaining. But I wonder why perfume makers haven't discovered wolverine musk. Don't they use skunk stuff for something like that?"

"I appoint you to look it up for a report," was Tom's answer.

The West High Science Fair in February was another Romig Junior High fair all over again, only this time the projects were much more sophisticated and they found competing with seniors considerably more stimulating. They spent the week before the fair typing a final summary. Each took a section of the report, added and subtracted, and finally, the day before the fair, neatly inserted it in a bound cover. Tom wired the pegboard backdrop to form sides and back and they covered one side with photographs of the animals at various stages; on the backboard in large, neat letters was the caption, "Wendy and Willy—A Study of Wolverine Behavior." Tom had built a cage to fit the very strict dimensions prescribed by science fair rules and both he and Pam were concerned the animals would be too restricted in the small space. To compensate for lack of space sideways, Tom built the cage upwards. The back was four feet high and the cage almost three feet high, though only 2 ½ feet wide.

"If they win this fair for us, we'll reward them with a day's run on the bluff," rationalized Tom.

"I think I'll need it as much as they," answered Pam. She was having her usual last minute woes getting the unruly kits fed and brushed.

Now one year old, their markings were very prominent, and Pam noted that Wendy's diamond was as white as Wilma's had been; Willy's stripes were the usual ivory color, however. She marveled at the mysteries of the genes that allowed Wendy to carry on her mother's characteristics. But she didn't marvel long. Wendy, reveling in the unaccustomed warmth of the house, decided a climb over the living room furniture would be an ideal morning adventure. Pam was glad her mother had gone shopping. She would have had a fit.

Somehow the project got packed into the rear of the station wagon and set up on time. The gymnasium of West High School was in the throes of the usual last-minute woes—mothers, fathers, students, pieces of plywood with legs walking down aisles, loud noises and tears. One sad boy was exhibiting his collection of molds despite the fact that a mouse had got into his project the night before and eaten most of his prize specimens. Pam and Tom felt sorry for him, but their own project soon regained their attention. Wendy and Willy were wild.

But wildest of all were Pam and Tom when their project again won them a first in the local school fair and another first in the Anchorage Fair, making them eligible for the regional event. Tom pulled Pam out into a deserted side hall and kissed her with enthusiasm. Pam was so excited by the victory of the evening, she couldn't stop babbling.

"Isn't it wonderful Tom? Now we can work on the regional. Oh, I want to go to Fort Worth so bad."

Just then Mr. Marx opened the door to the hall. "Hey, the Science Fair is in here," he teased. The two students were delighted to see him, and they shared memories once more. "Funny," he said, "but I was rather interested in a certain project over here. Otherwise, I wouldn't dream of coming to a *senior* high school. Seems like congratulations are getting a little routine with you two—but here's mine again." And he shook their hands warmly.

During the month between the two fairs, Tom and Pam consulted with their friend Bob Rausch. They had learned since the day on the porch that he had done considerable research on the wolverine along with its co-predators, the wolf and coyote. The two students realized then how much work and research went into the formation of fish and game policies and that Outside conservationists were really not justified in claiming that Alaskans were frittering away their natural resources without any thought of proper management.

His prediction that their unique research would win a first hands down in the regional fair came true. With a procedure that was no less hectic, though almost routine, they once more came through with flying blue and were beside themselves when they learned that Mr. Marx, a science fair officer, would chaperone their Fort Worth trip.

And what a trip that would be! Was Texas really ready for them?

Eleven

"Did you remember to tape the feeding instructions on the cage?" worried Pam.

"Yes, and I also put lots of 'Handle With Care' labels all over the box," assured Tom.

"Won't they get cold in the freight compartment?" asked Pam.

"I'm sure the airlines have been carrying animals for some time, and they don't seem to be freezing any," Tom said.

They were waiting at Gate 4, Anchorage International Airport. Mr. Marx joined them.

"Hi kids. Got your animals checked in?"

"Yeah, and Pam's worried they'll freeze to death in the baggage compartment. Hey, aren't you early Mr. Marx? I thought a big shot like you would come strolling out on the field as they pulled up the stairs."

"Don't kid yourself. I'm as excited as you kids. The price of an airline ticket to the Lower 48 isn't loose change, you know."

The older Walkers and Learners who had been coffeeing in the cafeteria joined them. Mr. Walker and Mr. Lerner had taken time off from work for the notable occasion. Joe and Tim, the other two student winners, and their goodbye parties arrived minutes later.

The loudspeaker blared. "Northwest Airlines announces the departure of its Flight 10 to Seattle/Tacoma. Now leaving, Gate 4."

There was a flurry of goodbye kisses and reminders before the entourage walked across the field and up the stairs into the Boeing jet.

Pam glanced anxiously to the freight loading cart under the plane but caught no reassuring sign of her fellow travelers.

After many questions and 9,000 miles of walking in the Seattle airport, she did sneak in a visit with Wendy and Willy in the baggage room. She unlocked the sliding door of the cage and gave them water. They let her know they enjoyed her reassuring voice and petting and struggled to get through the hole from which her hand reached. She toyed with the idea of walking them but realized their leashes were in her hand baggage in the terminal. The baggage attendants were very interested in the animals and told her they would keep a close eye on the two until they were put on the next plane to Dallas.

She found the group in the dining room of the airport.

"They don't seem to be minding too much," she replied to their questions. "How soon does our plane leave?"

"They should be calling it any minute. It's about 3 ½ hours to Love Field in Dallas. Then we transfer to a limo for the ride to Fort Worth," explained Mr. Marx.

Despite the light bantering of her fellow travelers, a captivating movie, and some tasty snacks, Pam couldn't erase her nagging concern for the wolverines. She led the group off the plane when they landed. The Alaskan group, composed of Pam, Tom, Tam, Joe, Tim, and Mr. Marx, was totally and completely awed by the vastness of the Texas terminal but even more by the milling of hordes of people. Half the world seemed to be traveling through Texas today. A Texas oilman who had chatted with them on the plane overheard their remarks and commented, "If you think this is bad, you should go through O'Hare in Chicago."

"I guess that's one thing we can be happy for in Alaska," said Mr. Marx. "We still have some space to move around in… that's not filled with people that is."

They were quick to note that the terminal was air conditioned, a fact of environment almost unknown in Alaska's seventy degree summers. They strolled down the long Branif wing of the airport, not a little affected by the rushing mobs around them. It was Tom who first noticed the ceiling.

"Get a load of that roof. Isn't that a crackup. That lime green reminds me of you in a jump suit," he said flirtatiously.

"Shocking pink isn't too far off from orange, either. For your information, those are Branif Airline colors. Emilio Pucci designed the hostess uniforms and they use the same colors for them," said the fashion expert with the group.

"Pucci? Who's he?"

"Oh never mind, ignorant."

Almost imperceptibly they had picked up the tempo of the rushing crowds around them, and before they reached the lower level, they were walking as fast as the others. Pam's concern for Wendy and Willy prodded them in the direction of the incoming freight and baggage room. They watched the circular conveyer spit out luggage and caught theirs when it appeared.

"Let's get over to the freight office now before Pam expires," said Mr. Marx.

After three wrong starts, they did find the freight department and presented the claim check. The descent had been particularly bumpy and Pam wondered if their stomachs were as upside down as hers. She was the first to spy the huge crate coming in on a conveyor belt, and the first to note that the door on the top had somehow unlatched and slid open. She held her breath, not daring to speak. Her eyes widened in horror as she saw Willy sniff curiously at the opening, then rear his head right through the hole. At this point, all eyes converged on the protruding head. Mr. Marx yelled first.

"Watch that animal! He's going to get out!"

But Willy had seen Pam. He scrambled out of the box and darted on to the conveyor belt. This moving contraption was not part of the Alaska scene and he snarled briefly then decided to get off fast. He started in the general direction of Pam, but the shouting onlookers thoroughly frightened him. Willy was traveling and he didn't care where.

Years later when Pam remembered all she could think of was one of those Mack Sennett silent movies she had seen on television.

Willy shifted into high gear and bounced off down the terminal through a maze of Texas boots and sandals. It was uncanny how fast those legs sidetracked when the top side registered the small fury in their midst.

"My gosh, he's heading for the escalator," screamed Pam.

"Catch him," Mr. Marx yelled to no one in particular.

Willy, noting that there weren't as many frightening legs on the down escalator, chose that path of least resistance and bounded up the down escalator. The few obstacles in his way also produced shrieks. Pam had darted up the ascending escalator hoping to head off Willy at the top. She pushed past other passengers in a frenzy, excusing herself all the way and at the same time trying to note Willy's progress on the opposite stairs. Whenever she saw some passenger lurch unexpectedly, she had a good idea as to that progress and he was gaining on her. She reached the top of the stairs just in time to see Willy dart off with a twenty foot lead. Tom came huffing behind her and joined the chase. They were off again. This time Willy veered to the right and sped along the wall where there were fewer of those noisy legs. The obvious happened. There was an open door and Willy did not bother to read the sign. "Ladies, Damen, Frauen" it spelled out. The door swung shut.

"Pam, he's gone into the ladies' room. Now's your chance to tackle him."

"Thanks a lot," she gasped.

The door did not open—it exploded. "Hilfe, hilfe, Mein Gott, ein wildes Beest!" And the white-faced Fraulein gasped her way to a bench where she struggled to avoid fainting. The exodus from the ladies' room continued, an international panorama of thoroughly distraught females. Pam finally got through the door and was not prepared for the sight which met her eyes. Willy was crouched in a corner snarling in absolute uncontrolled fury and fright, and balancing precariously atop a sink was a Texas matron, mink stole dangling, hat awry. The strong odor of a very familiar scent filled the room.

"Willy, Willy, stop it—calm down, that's a nice boy," and her voice cajoled, pleaded, soothed. The sound had a remarkable effect on Willy. She was soon able to touch him, then carry him out to the terminal. Mr. Marx was waiting with the leash. They snapped it quickly. Mr. Marx sniffed. They decided to move—fast.

They had no trouble hurrying the freight attendant into releasing Wendy, and she was joined by a much-traveled Willy in the cage. A somewhat reluctant red cap provided a cart and they moved to the limousine dispatch center just as some security police appeared down the hall.

"I suggest we get out of here fast," said Mr. Marx. They purchased limousine tickets.

"How many?" asked the bored clerk.

"Three adults, two children," answered Mr. Marx.

And they fled through the door to the limousine waiting outside.

"Quick, take the animals out of the cage and leash them," instructed Mr. Marx.

"I'll take care of the cage."

Tom grabbed Wendy and Pam took Willy. Before the startled driver could protest, they boarded the bus, handed them their tickets and raced to the rear of the bus. They noticed the bus driver was sniffing inquiringly. Outside, Mr. Marx was not doing as well.

"Y'all can't put that thing in here," the dispatcher complained. "It's too big. I won't have room for anyone else's baggage."

"There don't seem to be many other passengers," the teacher pleaded. "This is very important to us. We've come all the way from Alaska and we've heard so much about Texas hospitality. Sure hope you won't disappoint us." Then, something from an old movie must have come to mind. He handed the dispatcher a five dollar bill. Texas hospitality bloomed. The dispatcher allowed that maybe he could find room for the cage and it disappeared in the bowels of the bus. Mr. Marx rushed into the bus just as two security officers strolled through the door of the terminal and casually looked around.

"I just blew two week's worth of lunch money," he said to the waiting students. "If you two so much as dare to take one finger off those animals, I'm putting you on the next plane back to Anchorage." He sat down hard and took off his glasses. The trip was remarkably free of conversation for several miles. But the excitement simply could not be repressed. There was a beginning giggle from Pam. A snicker from Tom. And the motley crew burst into a roar of laughter that might have been heard ten miles away in Fort Worth.

Encouraged, the bus driver explained that this expressway was called the Mashers or Mixers or something like that and before they could question, he pointed out the Six Flags of Texas.

"What is it?" asked Pam pointedly.

"An amusement park, like Disneyland," the driver called back.

The group noticed the skyscrapers, the endless spans of concrete, pavement and steel. They observed the cobbled streets and that some building fronts appeared definitely Victorian, as though Fort Worth had been around a few years.

"How big is Fort Worth?" asked Joe.

"About 200,000," replied the driver. "Dallas is about 300,000."

"Don't tell him Anchorage is Alaska's largest city and it's only 50,000," whispered Tom to Joe. "They've got more people in Dallas that we have in all Alaska, and we could put two of Texas in the state of Alaska."

"Now for heaven's sake don't be telling everybody that, or they'll be thinking we're Alaska showoffs," admonished Pam.

"Y'all afraid to advertise?" mimicked Tom, already picking up the contagious drawl they had heard along the route.

They craned their necks like any tourist the remaining sixteen miles. The limousine dropped them right in front of their motel, and Pam and Tom tried to remain inconspicuous while Mr. Marx checked in and arranged for a place to keep the animals. They were relieved to find the desk clerk very cooperative. He showed them to a storage room where they could leave the cage and visit their pets as often as they wished. The clerk did politely suggest that the animals not be allowed in the rooms. Wendy and Willy were allowed to help them inspect the very blue swimming pool. They could not help but note the curious glances from poolside guests. When one fattish, bald type reared in his chair and sniffed, Mr. Marx decided Wendy and Willy needed a cage-type rest. About the same time the group became very much aware of the hot, humid 90-degree temperature. Pam located her room and the other four, sharing doubles, soon disappeared inside their doors. The boys were into bathing suits and out in the pool in minutes. When Pam emerged some time later, she noted Mr. Marx in swim trunks stretched flat in a pool-side lounge chair. On the small table beside him was a large, foaming mug of root beer.

———•◦•———

After the first day of drowsiness brought on by a five-hour time change, the party of five recuperated and became ambitious to explore the city. They wasted no time in visiting any point of interest suggested from botanical garden and museum to General Motors and Bell Laboratories. By the time the Science Fair opened on Monday, they were telling other visitors what to see. Early Monday morning, the group met in the motel lobby, then taxied to Tarrant City Center. This modernistic, concrete-domed structure would see a lot of them during the week. They awed over the landscaped entrance and moved inside. Tom could not believe his eyes when he looked at the vast floor. Though 400 project spaces had been set up, they covered only a fraction of the total floor space. There was a decided international flavor to the scene as the sound of foreign tongues reached them. Students from Germany, Japan, Austria, Switzerland, Paraguay, Brazil, Peru, and Puerto Rico would be entering exhibits. Right now, the hurly burly scene was very reminiscent of the science fair scene back home, and it was just as easy to get excited in German or Japanese as English. Tom noted one difference.

"Hey, get a load of the fancy dans in the Edwardian get up." And it was apparent that the European contingent was somewhat uniquely dressed in the current Carnaby Street fashion. The boys and girls from most of the other countries looked like anyone else from Smalltown, U.S.A.

Pam questioned, "Mr. Marx, how are the entrants selected for this fair? I mean, can anybody just come?"

"No, it's sponsored by the Science Service Club of America, in New York City, and any city or country school requesting entry in the International Fair must pay a $100 membership fee. That's all—no other red tape."

"Who decides where it will be held?"

"I'm not exactly certain, but I suppose it is bid on just like any other convention, and the bidder must be sure he has the facilities to house the exhibits as well as the crowd. The year before last it was held in Detroit, and next year it will go to San Francisco."

The group wandered through the sections noting the categories. They were not much different than home—zoological, botany, medicine and health, and biochemistry. The physics division contained the usual sections on applied physics, pure physics, chemistry, earth and space mathematics.

Pam and Tom returned to the information desk and determined the procedure necessary to set up their exhibit. They completed the entry blank and picked up a schedule.

"Man, this is sure more complicated than the fair at home. Look, we get two days to set up the exhibit, that's Monday and Tuesday."

"What happens on Wednesday—oh, here it is. We have to be with our projects on Wednesday afternoon. That's scary. What if the judge asks a question we can't answer?" worried Pam.

"Don't answer it, that's all," concluded Tom. "They finish the judging Thursday morning. Hey, look at Thursday night. That's neat. There's a dance at the Alamo Hotel."

"What I'll really be waiting for is the Awards Banquet on Friday. You know, Tom, they don't pin blue ribbons on exhibits here. You just have to suffer until they make the announcements at the dinner."

The group wandered through the aisles and found their designated sections. Some early birds had already set up, and the group began to feel uneasy. They sensed that they were among the truly elite, and their individual projects suddenly paled in comparison.

They returned to the motel and once more found themselves in the frenzy of getting to the fair on time. This time, with no mother-chauffeured station wagon, they had the added hassle of convincing a taxi driver that he would not be attacked by wild animals from Alaska. Mr. Marx again played cage carrier, but this time he rented a U-Haul. Pam couldn't determine whether he was triumphant or turbulent when she saw him struggle into the center with the enclosure. She and Tom unburdened him. They set up the backboard and as soon as they had the cage in place, they untied Willy and Wendy from the table legs and locked them securely on display.

"Please, please don't get excited and smell up the place," prayed Pam. Wendy whined protestingly then decided all was in vain and snuggled down against Willy. A crowd gathered to watch and the five found themselves an Alaska Chamber of Commerce for at least half an hour. After they had refuted the igloo fantasy for the 9,000th time, Mr. Marx remarked loudly, "Well, we have to get back to our igloo now." To the assembled group he explained, "We had one sent down in a refrigerated ship so we could stay cool in this hot weather."

"You always leave 'em laughing, don't you Mr. Marx?" said Tom as they descended the stairs of the Center.

"Try being funny, next time," added Pam.

———•◦•———

By Wednesday morning tension had mounted to the point where Mr. Marx spent most of his time thinking up things for the students to do. A couple races in the swimming pool eased things, but then Pam left saying she had to set her hair in rollers for the afternoon appearance. Mr. Marx took the boys out for a super-size malted milk and they wandered in and out of stores to kill time. They were back in time to dress and be at the Center by 1:00 pm. Pam could not remember when she'd been so breathless. She and Tom took up positions near their exhibit, and the other boys went off to theirs. Pam tidied the cage and rearranged pictures nervously. She was relieved when she saw the judges turn the corner at the end of their aisle. The agony would soon be over. She became much more relaxed when she sensed that the judges were very interested in Wendy and Willy, and asked lots of questions about Alaska as well. Pam made it a point to emphasize how little research had been done on the wolverine. She ended with a bit of politicking. She invited the judges to Alaska for some real fishing.

The group dawdled away Thursday, then spent several hours being lost and trying to find the Alamo Hotel. The dance music reached them before they reached it. Mr. Marx covered both ears and walked upstairs with them. Before he could even adjust his eyes to the darkness inside, Tom was dancing two feet away from Pam and said, "I'll be downstairs. Don't any of you leave this room before I get back. Got it?"

"Shucks. Thought we'd be able to get away from you," teased Tom, shuffling his feet, swiveling his hips and moving his bended elbows close to his side. "This music is cool. Isn't it Mr. Marx?"

"Yeah, it leaves me cold all right. Remember what I said." And he disappeared. Later that night, the group returned intact and not badly damaged by their brush with international society. The most important day was yet to come.

On Friday evening, they were among the first to present their tickets and enter the large dining room of the hotel. They searched out and found their table, and waited for the climax of the evening. For once food wasn't important to Tom, and he scarcely remembered what he'd eaten. Pam betrayed her nervousness by giggling more than usual. They examined the head table and Mr. Marx pointed out various dignitaries. Then the suspense began. The master of ceremonies began to call names and smiling students marched up to receive medals or plaques or other awards. Tom reached for Pam's hand under the table and squeezed so hard she winced. The zoology section was one of the last to be announced in the biology division.

"Third prize, Zoology, Mr. Hans Metzger, Austria." The crowd applauded as Hans moved forward. Tom squeezed again and Pam jiggled in her chair.

"Second prize," intoned the MC, and the two leaned forward. "Miss Elaine Sweet, Atlanta, Georgia." Pam stopped breathing, and covered her face with her hands. "First Prize, Zoology, goes to"—and there was an eternity of hesitation as he read the card handed to him, "Miss Pam Walker and Mr. Tom Lerner, from Anchorage, Alaska." Dazed, the two walked through the applauding crowd, accepted their medals, turned to have their pictures taken, and somehow returned to the table. Mr. Marx's grin was about to split his face. It was cliché, but he said it anyway. "Congratulations, Kids." Pam wondered if she ever again would be quite as excited.

Twelve

Late in May, Tom told Pam. The FAA was transferring his dad to the Lower 48 sometime in August. Pam found it difficult to comprehend an existence without Tom. While their parents frowned on any reference to going steady at their ages, they had grown very fond of one another. Their mutual concern over Wendy and Willy served as a bond, but their personalities had also meshed on an intellectual and emotional level. They liked each other very much. They missed the bus on purpose one night and walked home together."

"Tom, I don't even want to think about it. It's too awful."

"It'll be rough for me, too, Pam. I'll miss you too. Maybe we can pick colleges close to each other. Or maybe I can come up here to work in the summer time. One thing for sure, I'm coming back to Alaska when I graduate from college. Think you'll still be around then, Pam?" he asked, suddenly shy.

"That's a safe bet," she answered softly.

They crossed the Alaska Railroad tracks then cut into the woods near home. They followed a worn path through the woods.

"What will happen to Wendy and Willy?" Tom asked after a silence.

"I'm kind of worried about that. They are getting to be a lot of work... the straw on the floor could be changed twice a day if I had the time. And that stuff costs two dollars a bale at the feed store. I've offered my little brothers a good price to cut it down by the bluff, but they get tired after about a quarter's worth. I can still get meat and vegetable trimmings at the Safeway but it's a lot of work to get there

WILMA

before the rabbit owners. I tried freezing the meat in small bags and that worked well. But it's sure lots of work, especially with finals coming up and the homework they've been piling on. I'm about to crack."

"So what are you saying?"

"I just don't know, Tom… what do you think we should do about Wendy and Willy?"

"We could always give them back to the zoo."

"I thought of that too, but then I think of that Canadian who did all the research on wolverines and remember he said they were suppressed by captivity."

"Then what you really mean is we should take them back to the woods?"

"I'd just hate to give them up, Tom. It's worse than having a pet dog put to sleep or losing a cat. Wendy and Willy are—well, almost part of the family. I guess I love them just as much as family."

"Want me to go with you if we take them back?"

"I couldn't do it without you, Tom. But let's not go until the last minute. Summer is almost here and I won't be so busy with studies then. Let's get our folks to go up sometime in August, okay?"

And the pact was made.

Before school was out, they walked over to Romig Junior High and informed Mr. Marx of their decision. He made them feel better when he agreed and said they had really learned about all they could, because to his knowledge wolverines had never bred in captivity.

"They are yearlings now and should be ready to breed about August or September. You might even be able to spot them in later winters or summers, which reminds me, why don't you have them tagged by Fish and Game?"

"Let's," said Pam enthusiastically, glad that the doors would not be forever closed.

About the middle of August, Tom and Pam loaded the pets into the Lerner station wagon and Tom's Dad drove them to Caribou Creek. They had decided to leave the animals on the opposite side of the river

124

in the Game Refuge. This would keep them out of Wilma's territory and give them time to develop wilderness wariness in a safer environment. Tom's Dad crossed the creek, then turned a sharp left into a campground on the river's bank. Wendy and Willy were leashed. The teenagers searched for the familiar yellow BLM marker which would tell them where to enter the public access trail. Pam spied it first.

"Think I'll try a little fishing while you're up there," said Tom's Dad. "There probably won't be a thing in this muddy glacier water, but at least I can practice casting."

The trail was steep and zigzagged right and left. Even Wendy and Willy were puffing when they reached a resting place. With the moment of goodbye coming closer, Pam hugged Wendy to her and softly petted the velvet back. Willy, jealous, moved over to get his fair share. She hugged him too and her eyes blurred. Tom turned away and stared hard at a distant spruce.

They continued up the mountain and reached a stream. It was trickling down, falling in short waterfalls to stone pools on its way to the roaring stream far below.

"This looks like something out of a movie," exclaimed Pam. "It almost looks fake, it's so perfect." She looked downstream at the branches bending over the water.

"Isn't it funny that this side of the river is so rocky and sandy and the other is all muskeg and bushes? No wonder sheep like this refuge. Hope our wolverines do too."

Wendy and Willy had a great time first lapping the water, then splashing through it. Tom unhooked their leashes. Wendy sniffed her way into the bushes. In a matter of seconds they saw her nosing a small hold in the bank and were startled to see her return with a small hare in her mouth.

"I don't know why I worried about you Wendy," observed Pam. "I should have let you do your own hunting a long time ago."

Willy decided to play one of his games. He grabbed the leash Tom had tossed to the ground and ran off into the woods. Tom chased, and when Willy saw Tom stop, he stopped. Tom pretended to start again and off went Willy. The game continued for ten minutes and Tom came back to fling himself on the bank beside Pam.

"Watch to see if he comes back," whispered Tom. Sure enough, it was only minutes before Willy was rubbing against Tom's leg. He rested for a few minutes, then suddenly reared his hind legs and wafted the air. Tom and Pam reared too to see what was attracting him. They raced up to a ridge and watched him lope off down stream. Far below on the opposite bank of the ravine they could see a wolverine busily enjoying a meal. Willy needed no blueprint. They surmised that she might be a female in season. They last saw their small friend aggressively pursuing the object of his affection and turned quietly back to the trail.

Wendy had finished her meal and decided to explore further. They watched her head up trail and once she swiveled her neck in that humorous way they had come to know so well—as if to say farewell. Holding back tears, the teenagers turned down hill. The late summer sun went under a cloud and a chilly breeze rustled the leaves. They stopped by the stream, and Tom pulled Pam to him. She buried her face in his sweatshirt and sobbed quietly.

Then she whispered, "Goodbye Wendy and Willy. And Tom."

Epilogue

In late summers when Pam passed by, she would gaze up at the spruce-covered slopes above Caribou Creek and remember her first loves. Somehow those soft furry balls would be forever associated with the softness of a first kiss. She knew Tom would come back to this Alaska they both loved. Outsiders accused Alaskans of being eternal optimists and she wasn't about to disappoint them. For now she would drink deeply of all it had to offer—and that was plenty!